CW00742897

The North is a publication of

the poetry business

The magazine is published twice a year.

Edited by Ann Sansom and Peter Sansom with Suzannah Evans

Designed & typeset by Utter Design utter.co.uk.
Cover montage by Utter from photos by Jamie Street and
Tom Wheatley found on Unsplash.
Printed by Page Bros.

We are currently only considering work submitted online
(not by post). Please go to www.poetrybusiness.co.uk/about/
submissions/ for more details.

We are grateful for the financial assistance of
Arts Council England.

Distributed by BookSource, 50 Cambuslang Road,
Cambuslang Investment Park, Glasgow G32 8NB.

Advertising rates on request.

Subscribe to *The North*

Current rate is £22 per annum or £44 for two years (digital
version £16/£22), single copies £12 (digital version £9)
(overseas print subscription £28 per annum or £56 for two
years, single copies £14).

✂

Subscription address:
The Poetry Business,
Campo House, 54 Campo Lane
Sheffield S1 2EG tel 0114 4384074.
www.poetrybusiness.co.uk/product-category/the-north/
subscriptions/

✂

Correspondence address:
email: office@poetrybusiness.co.uk

✂

Please make cheques etc. payable to The Poetry Business

www.poetrybusiness.co.uk

N69 POETRY

150 POEMS BY 81 POETS

Jon McLeod

Peter Sirr

Gary Allen

Susan Bedford

Liz Byrne

Joe Caldwell

Kath McKay

Tom Weir

Yvonne Green

Peter Daniels

Rosie Garland

Robert Hamberger

Victoria Gatehouse

Alan Payne

Jo Peters

Maggie Reed

Karl Riordan

Penelope Shuttle

Mara Bergman

Rod Whitworth

Maria Ferguson

Paul Mills

Kate Rutter

John McAuliffe

Steph Morris

Ed Reiss

Shash Trevett

John Harvey

Paula Cunningham

Martin Reed

Georgia Conlon

Peter Knaggs

Barbara Marsh

Nigel Pantling

Charlotte Gann

John Goodby

Heidi Williamson

David Underdown

Aziz Dixon

Kayleigh Campbell

Faith Lawrence

Marilyn Longstaff

Sarah Mnatzaganian

Kelly Creighton

Matthew Paul

Fokkina McDonnell

Susanna Harding

Chris Jones

Rebecca Farmer

Rachel Davies

Lydia Macpherson

Rachel Burns

Emma Simon

Jean Stevens

Mary Matusz

Rebecca Green

Michael Schmidt

Richard Evans

Carson Wolfe

Pam Thompson

Anna Woodford
& Tara Bergin

Helen Angell

Safia Khan

Marion New

Elizabeth Gibson

Serena Alagappan

Tom Branfoot

Beth Davies

Chloe Elliott

Karen Downs-Barton

Jon Miller

Zoë Walkington

Luke Samuel Yates

Aazhiyaal

Romesh Gunasekera

Wimal Dissanayake

Anne Ranasinghe

Mahakavi

Richard de Zoysa

Cliff Yates

**For A Full List Of Poems
Please See Back Pages**

N69 PROSE

EDITORIAL

Welcome to the latest issue. The first available as an ebook – let us know if you'd like to subscribe that way (more convenient, cheaper), a step we've taken not least because of the crazy postage situation in Europe. But also for the rather stylish portability. Poetry books are often (especially ours) lovely design objects, but there's a pleasure in having a version always to hand, and incidentally it solves at a click the perennial small press problem of *distribution*. (Just so you know, all our latest publications, even the smallest pamphlets, are available as ebooks.)

The ebook *North* anyway, to be clear, is separate to another initiative, *East of The North*, which is an online offshoot that we're putting together in the coming weeks. It will include a deal of archive material as well as trailers from each latest issue and, crucially, audio and video, so it is in essence *The North* cubed. It will also be free of charge. We know that you will see *EoTN* as a bonus rather than an alternative to subscribing.

The previous issue was brilliantly guest-edited by Andrew McMillan and Stephanie Sy-Quoia. It took the unheard-of approach of choosing one poem each by 100 poets. This latest is more conventionally unusual – having just as many strong and surprising poems, many singletons again, but also short sets, all of which amount we hope to a varied but coherent read. With, in among, those three-dimensional experiences that a poem can bring when it speaks genuinely to or through us.In any event, Ann and I very much enjoyed putting the issue together, not least because of the quality of so many of the submissions. Though it's true that you can have too much of a good thing – there were over a thousand for us to read in two already particularly busy months.

Among other diversions at that time (please see the PB website) are our rather wonderful digital Poets in Residence, and a very special programme of guest-tutored digital workshops. Also, the New Poets Prize and the International Book & Pamphlet competitions – two years of which are featured in the current issue: that is, the announcement of the 2023 winners, and a feature devoted to the 2022 quartet, whose outstanding collections are now edited and published and who each have written the 'Poets I Go Back To' this time. (Poems by the 2023 winners will feature in *EoTN* and in the next print issue.)

In the current issue too we're glad to say is the 'Featured Title' anthology, *Out of Sri Lanka* from Bloodaxe; also another excellent 'Blind Criticism' and (though we don't take them for granted) the usual high standard of reviews of notable recent books and pamphlets. These were mostly commissioned by our assistant editor, Suzannah Evans, who has taken on more teaching and so will work for us only occasionally now. Likewise, we're sorry to say it was the right time for Ellen, our Co-Director and business manager and Katie (production and marketing) to leave the Poetry Business. They were wonderful to work with and made a difference to almost every aspect of the Poetry Business -- they will be greatly missed. Happily we have taken on two excellent new members of staff in Jess and Pete, though, as is the way of things, doing fewer hours. In addition we have put behind us a wrong-headed HMRC claim that would have closed us down and which has taken us (and our accountants and board) three outraged and stressful years to appeal against. We are currently waiting for our latest funding bid to be considered by the Arts Council, themselves of course under pressure. But with any luck we are now moving forward again.

However, this editorial draws to a sombre close because of two other features here, about our friends the poets John Foggin and Gina Wilson, whom you may know have died. And as I write, we know that many of you like us will have been shocked and saddened by the recent death of Gboyega Odubanjo.We were fortunate in having Gboyega work at the Poetry Business for a while with Suzannah as an assistant editor. He was also one of our New Poets, whose pamphlet, *Aunty Uncle Poems,* won the Michael Marks Award a couple of years ago, and whose first full-length collection, *Adam,* is forthcoming from Faber. A foundation is being set up by his family and friends in his honour.

The Quaker Path

Come, let's take the Quaker path through the unhitched gate.
Let's wait a moment in the half-tunnel of hawthorns

and peer through the clouded windows of a static caravan.
Best now, in May. The sedge warbler's clicks and catches.

People came here on way to meeting,
dressed in the perfect piebald of oystercatchers.

Sometimes there is a hare. Black ear tips risen
above the wheat spikes. Listen until we have passed.

Ages

What am I, ten?
The train crosses the sparkling river;
in a hotel across from the station
my grandmother hands me a glass of stout.
My lips are black with summer.

What am I, fifteen?
We've walked the length of the city
and must have talked forever
but all that's left of desire
is the peach I bought her just here.

What am I, twenty-five?
The ice hangs in the trees,
the skaters race through the towns.
On the balcony, beyond the stuck door,
my frozen lives wait for the thaw.

What am I, fifty-nine?
The sun streams in on the table
where all of us are feasting
expectant as apostles
on the last of the bread, the last of the wine.

What am I, a hundred and three?
The cold air plays on the earth.
If someone should think of me
a blade of grass will stop in its tracks,
a leaf curl in mid-flight.

One word poem

If you follow the embankment
that once ran steam trains behind the backs of the terraced houses
between Belfast and Derry and the sprawling rows

of the new graveyard and the housing estates

my father's racing pages
my mother's broken line of ragged washing

and the back bedrooms where the last thing
the old and dying see

are their breaths and the water stains,

you come out to a full-stop
a half-demolished railway bridge
shrouded in barbed wire and brambles and tribal wisdom

that gives you the names of those who are gone
but who loved one another for a few vague moments

who held the bridge as their own
like the promises that life gives on late

insect summer evenings
beer-bottle caps studded like manifestos into the soft

crumbling cement,

in your mind
you find you have already left

for a world that is no bigger than a shelled pea

or the words that were painted high up on the half-span
by an unknown hand in a mirror image
one word falling into nothing, Fuck.

The philosophers

Our form teacher called us the shit-house philosophers
academic fugitives hanging out in the school toilets
with its high frosted windows and last summer's fossilised insects
the smell of Harpic emptied down toilet bowls
and blue disinfectant cubes in the urinals

solemn over half butts and nicked singles
telling dirty jokes and misinformation about girls
looking at the unfolded pages ripped out in a hurry
from older brother's hidden porno mags

copying last minute homeworks
intimidating younger boys for dinner money
arranging after school fights with the boys from St. Pat's
how to make workable guns in the metal workshop –

how vulnerable it is to be alone
a voice without babble
and then the present hangs between space and time
and the other dimension known but forgotten by us all

no bigger or of any more importance than the dust motes
like broken skin or unwashed bodies
spiralling in the sun shafts of winter light
from the fractured sky-lights that open endlessly into the blue.

Saturday night

When the taxi came, idling outside,
its engine chugging away *at that time in the morning*

I wanted to pretend it was for next door's,
collecting and taking home laughter and whooping-it-up,
finally leaving quiet across the party wall.

Outside, some driver on double time –
one who can take care of clubbers in not enough clothes,
who likes night work
and the occasional run to Manchester

our transport to you,
lying on a bed with the light on
immeasurably still.

Mental Health Service

I don't miss the waiting-list, files marked urgent,
weekly reports of numbers waiting, longest wait,
latest targets, how we fail to meet them.

I don't miss Critical Incident Enquiries seeking blame,
the myth that risk is a shark which can be tamed;
darkness eliminated; rain sent back to the sky.

I don't miss sleepless nights, worry
about those who walk the knife-edge, rope-edge
between living and dying.

I miss a quiet room, half-open blinds,
clock ticking, two people breathing,
words and the space   between   words.

I want to go back to that school

sit at a desk in a room full of desks,
wait for my name to be called for a slap,
not walk to the front, not hold my hand out;

go to the toilet and not hide in a cubicle,
feet drawn up so I'm invisible, not hold
my breath while Sr. Cecilia walks past;

walk across the hockey pitch, not cower
behind a tree, legs cold-mottled and bruised,
not ever being chosen for the team;

sit on that chair outside the head-nun's office,
not waiting for my punishment, not crying
and wiping snot, not humiliated;

stay for lunch, not eat brown soup made of tails,
white bread dusted with mould, not walk
around the hall, balancing a book on my head.

I want to go back to that school and it
not be there, but it is.

JOE CALDWELL

As we drove down, the reservoir was fuller

than this time last year. The machine's broken
so it's free parking. The camera looks down
benignly as we trudge up the path.
It's spring and dad still loves commenting
on the depth of the reservoir. One of us
holds a gate for the others. One of us
makes a joke about bank holiday weather.
We offer our good mornings to the grey faces
coming down from the opposite direction.
We are still climbing the same green hill.

KATH McKAY

Nackedei

The winter solstice, and I wanted to walk in the park on the shortest day. Or at least make a bonfire in the garden, light candles against the dark and catch the year turning.

But the children wouldn't go out in the cold. Instead, they took their tops off, and ran round yelling 'Nackedei', the word brought back from Berlin, after seeing friends strip naked to swim in a lake. They tumbled over each other like circus clowns, all legs and arms, together and then apart. *Nackedei, Nackedei.* We made our own ritual: shout 'Nackedei' three times, circle round, then bellow '*Thank you for the light*'. Again and again, *Nackedei, Nackedei, Nackedei. Thank you for the light.* And we were thankful, as at 3.58 the day lengthened, and the stiffest of us felt that old stirring: the sun will return; Spring will come.

The trick, I'm told,

not to carry you close
but hold you tight –

though I'm not sure
what it is I hold some nights.

Some nights what I hold
is not a child

but a child's many parts.
Some nights what I carry

is not a child
but a child's fear of the dark.

Anchor

Some nights I imagine
your mother's body as the sea –
the tide-shift,

the push and pull of water,
and you as a boat caught in a storm
and nothing more.

It's easier that way –
to think of a stern rusting, a hull rotting,
not bone, not you.

Easier to think of a boat, not you,
coming to rest on the bed
of your mother's womb,

the echo of her pulse a sonar,
the sonographer a sailor
searching for any sign of life

worth guiding back to shore –
your tiny heartbeat, a pilot light
flickering behind a closed door.

Rain

We were told you should have been
developing a sense of the world outside the body

but were yet to learn about rain –
too soon to tell the difference

between your mother in the shower
and your mother caught in a storm

on her way back from the station,
too much distance between the womb

and the rain-soaked river.
But if we're going to talk about rain

I should probably mention the night
I found your mother in the dark,

as if the living room light
might frighten you.

And if we're going to talk about rain,
I should probably mention

the crackle of rain-on-a-rooftop rain
as they readied the machine,

then the quiet fuss of distant rain –
rain-on-the-radio rain,

rain-on-sand rain,
as the machine found its range.

Then the worry of too much rain,
then the worry of not enough rain

as they scoured the lake
of your mother's body

for the sound of your heart
and only static remained.

The Time Was Brutal

But the place wasn't,
Girls never went out

They were born at home
Carried in a covered litter

To their mother-in-laws'
Houses on their wedding

Days and only ever left to
Be buried. That was until

1920 when our child-bride grandmas
Became matriarchs who brought recipes

Language, gestures, customs,
Practices, in the boukhcha they

Bundled their degs, corpas,
Lingheries, Joma, the time

Was brutal for real then, although
It taught their children that it wasn't

As primitive as Boukhara had been,
Never colonised, they learned to turn

Their backs on some of their parents'
Ideas, to laugh even if they showed

Respect, at the throw-backs to a time,
Place, presence which couldn't travel,

Even if the smell of its food rumbled
Its grandhildren's bellies, the sound

Of endearments lullabied them, oh oh
I went back, 100 years after my grandparents

Left, when my father died, at 96, oh oh
Its beauty, manners, gentle and coarse,

Shrewd and generous landscape, its huge
Sweet grapes, melon, tutim, its raisin varieties

Long, gold, round, black, green, white-sacked
Its garinim, almonds, walnuts, pistaches Iranian,

Boukhari, its breads Tashkenti, Samarkandi –
Boukhara's Emir imported flour, water but

Couldn't emulate, bring me the air he laughed,
The Emirate a hundred years on was unchanged,

Stalin made the language eat itself, but the history
My grandparents took onto our seder tables was

There, the gestures, smiles, pace, crudeness,
Civilities were visceral connections to myself,

In a time where to judge the past wasn't how
To show I've mastered the now, nor in a place

Of unearned sentiment (sentimental),
Geography tells the truth if you speak

Its languages, or listen to (remember)
Those who do

Alexandria

The Gemorah says Alexandria's synagogue was so big
There was a flag raised until the B'al tephilla stopped
And then lowered so the people at the back should know
It was time to say *Amen*

Kaleidoscope

Those who never saw Shanghai's covered market,
Which spread for acres, as so many starved,
Who never tasted the goodies cooked in the streets,
Who never saw the fishermen seeding the night,
While tombs steamed with coloured light,
Who never heard the low sound of our prayers,
The clash of Chinese New Year,
The cacophony of our languages,
Must remember that there are other places,
Times, ways to live.

Tetrissed

through   divorce
ensa   backgammoned

through stopped   work
Netflixed   through

lockdown   delegated
daughtering   mother

grandmaing housekeeping
never   shared

what lived then   the page
lines   the drawer

then the quiet   land
of   not-rejections

smiled over   websighted
blogged   like

the wheel-barrow   of
books   taken to

market   the reading-films
interviews   posted

essays   novelled
Lipkin   peer read

or mis-read   private
a love   which his
widow   understood

The Parasaurolophus

It ran on its two back legs, and its front legs were short,
but they say it could stand on them how a kangaroo can,
thirty-something feet to the end of its long thick tail.
Its feature was a prominent crest pointing backwards
over its neck. While other dinosaurs had solid bony crests,
with the usual reasons for crests – recognition as your species,
or as male (males must be seen to be male) –
this bony crest was in fact a special
luxurious hollow extension of its nasal sinuses.

Let the palaeontologists put it in the conditional –
'Parasaurolophus might have blown air through it
to trumpet the alarm'– but those inner cavities
would resonate, like feeding a prima donna's head voice
through a trombone, making a tuneful bellow
calling to the herd, the loved one, the child.
And why not call this hooting crest a horn
– it's not a horny horn, not keratin like a rhino's,
nor bony like an antler, but a horn to blow.

I too have nasal passages I can feel as they vibrate,
sounding through my nose into my head,
but I'd never match this unicorn's organ.
The New Mexico Museum of Natural History
has recorded simulated ancient air re-echoing
through a skull bigger than my whole body,
as I can tell from this display in South Kensington.
A puny human, I stand breathing before it,
the animal's crest as long as my two outstretched arms.

The seven last words

Father forgive them, for they know not what they do.

Good Friday. Christ is on the cross. My mother is on her knees,
grinding bare floorboards and wringing her hands.
Six pews back from the altar rail and its exclusive holiness,
she keeps vigil with the other quiet and desperate
church women who will not desert their Lord.

In the churchyard, the afternoon settles between the gravestones,
the air sick with wild garlic. The sun covers its face
in disbelief at the things men do. Like the time
her brothers took her into the woods,
tied her to a tree and left her.

Today shalt thou be with me in paradise.

Like beads, she counts off the times
her in-laws called her Fat Mary.
The years she learned to take a joke.
The make-do-and-mend. The one good coat.
The single cigarette after daily housework.

Woman, behold thy son. Behold thy mother.

Counts the times she's used the words
guilt, fault, shame. The whispered revulsion
of women priests. *Because we have the curse.*
Counting the total occurrences of *curse.*

My god, my god, why hast thou forsaken me?

The times her own mother said,
I couldn't stop having children, Mary. Why can't you start?
Counting the sum total of miscarriages.

I thirst.

The times she swallowed her father's wisdom:
it is worthier to do things you don't enjoy,
than things you do. And:
a woman with her skirt up can run faster
than a man with his trousers down.

It is finished.

Speeding her WAF ambulance along a runway
to salvage the remains of men from a burning Lancaster.
Her father's ship torpedoed by a U-Boat.
The V2 bomb-blast rubble of the street. Dear Christ,

the times I thought her silly because she wouldn't
watch films about shipwrecks, or get on planes.
Her terror that God would spew her from his mouth,
because thou art lukewarm, when all she was seeking
was a glimmer of mercy in outer darkness.

Into thy hands I commend my spirit.

Too late, I know the questions to ask,
the kindness I want to pour into the wounds.
Too late, I give thanks for her gift
of unfailing love, for her life
and its succession of small miracles
of persistence, her dogged faith
that if she prayed for long enough,
a stone would roll away.

The House of My Body

There's a hole in the roof where pigeons
roost with rain. I ache in my rafters,
creak through joists.
Who owns these spider-hammocks
crying out not to be disturbed?
Let them go about their business
(hunger, weaving, murder) while I'm
opening doors for my years.

In the bed of my breath
friends who died thirty years ago
speak large as life, and waking becomes
a subtle disappointment. My windows
shake their weathers outside. I marry
a dog to the lamp-post, a pillar-box
to scattering twigs, sweep my yard
of fag-ends, moss-clots, bus-tickets.

I garden the suck and shovel
of my dirt, grub through soil
where yellow returns like morning,
scarlet also, such flags against
surrender to my neighbours the slugs.
I say *nibble little*. I say *leaf and water
and flourish*. Celebrate my blossom,
achieve my grass, give steadfast
permission to my worms.

Red Door

When I told my mother she must go
into a home she said *I'll die then!*
as if her threat proved all she had
to bargain with was death.
The walls we'd stolen from her
tumbled past her cheek.
Her words couldn't link
to each other, though she understood
we were making her an old woman
in a home of old women who lost
their sons' names, but thought
those heads wore noses and ears
of boys who once jutted against
her hip, like jugs at a well –
cracking now into monstrous men who
make her forget she chose wallpaper,
painted ceilings.
                    Did I say *Mother,
don't die*? A laugh knocked itself
out of me, as if I'd bandaged
our burns, strapping her wrists
to her sides, so she wouldn't fly
over the park that bruised her orchid,
tarnished her necklace, buried
the keys to her flat, a red door
we found open most evenings
when the lake had swallowed her swans.

My First Crush was my Cardiologist

He asked was I on the pill / as he cold-pressed
the stethoscope beneath my left breast / I was fifteen

his eyes were on his watch / he was counting
under his breath / I didn't tell him / I'd never

been kissed / feared my wiring too / unstable /
my hair-trigger heart / its crimson jolts

of splashback on the ultrasound / He was the first
to listen for the quiet clicking / of my mitral valve

the one who told the GP it wasn't all in my head
the one to nick open a channel in my chest /

feed a wire through my veins / and jump-start /
it / out of me / that wild-hoof rhythm

no-one believed in / Afterwards / all gawky from
morphine / I was a rag doll Mum said she couldn't dress /

He came to me then / lowered himself to the tight /
edge of my hospital bed / slid down his mask

uncapped his fountain pen / Then he drew me my heart
inked crosses / to show where the faults lay

The Day Comes When I Can't Hear The Crickets

Late August   a walk across moorland
hawthorns shaped by the wind   earth stirred

                   to dust by my children's feet
         desire paths through heather
perfume kicked up   startling

the air as they make for the crag
              the valley flushed with a light
                        that's almost autumnal.

Listen they say   *listen*
and I'm standing so still   really straining

but it's beyond me now
the frequency of high summer –
              a remembered static in long grasses
lush-verged lanes, trilling –
              a campsite near Whitby

my brother and I   laughing
my mother standing so still
                   hair pushed back from her ears –

         all those tiny bones inside
         malleus   incus   stapes

fitting together like my bones
some intricate mechanism   beginning
                              to fail

and her kids thinking she's having them on
when she tells them she can't hear the crickets.

Red Skies

Marines billeted on our house
at the top of Market Hill,
my father insisting guns
are left at the door,
boots clattering up the stairs.

The view from Fort George:
roads blocked, plantations ablaze.

Beyond the harbour
HMS Devonshire,
and the man called Petit Père,
detained on Carriacou,
knowing the future was his.

Walking on Water

Crowds from all over the island
gathered on the Carenage,
drawn by Petit Père's promise
to walk on water
once the sun had set.

He appeared out of the dark,
his face dimly lit by a lamp,
the low-lying schooner
beneath his feet
barely visible.

As he drew close,
gliding over the silent sea,
his white jacket
shone like the moon;
in his hand a microphone.

Chuckles rippled along the shore;
up Cockroach Alley.
Above the harbour, men
in Richmond Hill Prison
had a bird's-eye view.

Petit Père's voice floated
up to Fort George.
My dear people,
the estate owners
would have me killed –

Richmond Hill Prison

At their windows, the men listened
to Petit Père's voice in the harbour.
When he said *Grenada's a prison*,
they stamped their feet. When he spoke
of Fédon's Rebellion, they cheered.
I'm not telling you to burn down
Mr John Brown's house.
But you know where it is –
In their cells, the prisoners grinned.
One wrote on the wall above his bed:

    Fédon come-back

    1795   1951

Spells

Rumours cobwebbed the island.
Petit Père was a mystic,
a Rosicrucian, an obeah-man.

Bones in his yard.
A black doll under his tree.
Folk who disappeared.

The most potent spell, though,
was the rise in wages
following the strike.

Women in cheap cotton dresses
cried out in the fields –
Petit Père teach we to wear panty!

Guava Cheese

Even the thugs in the Mongoose Gang
couldn't intimidate Widow Con.
When one smashed down her door
in Grenville, she looked him in the eye,
picked up a Coronation tin
with Queen Elizabeth on the lid –
This is for Petit Père. Some guava cheese.
The man looked at her, mouth open,
the cutlass in his hand hanging loose.
Tell him it's from Mrs Connolly,
who taught him the Queen's English
... when he was still in rags.

Fédon's Star

The last time Petit Père's tailor
climbed Morne Fédon
to watch the sun rise from the sea,
he knew his days were numbered.

From the summit, he observed
Fédon's pitiless star,
at midday, invincible,
before the swift blazing descent.

When Petit Père had claimed to be
Fédon's descendant,
as valiant as the sun,
the tailor called him an imposter.

After his death – the car he was driving
crashed near Gouyave –
there was talk of a falling-out.
Something about the price of a suit.

Abbess

at dusk
still as stone
in the doorway
under the turf lintel
wild winging thoughts
blackly
swirl grief
settle into solace
not lost
flown to rest
what she owes
she pays
thrusts anguish out
Aidan's gone home
she says
she tells herself
not lost to me
not lost

Almassera, June 2016

Voice clamour
distant thunder

a lorry squeezes down narrow streets in Relleu
chink of crockery as breakfast is cleared.

cockerel
　　　　swallow
　　　　　　　chuckle of hens

The murmur by the pool, sparrows glitter
the valley, clouds buff a sandy haze over hills.

Beekeeper in white tends hives
across the ravine; his dog yelps.

Cockerel crows
　　　　swallows slide
　　　　　　　skim the pool
　　　　　　　　　　circle around twittering.

High in the sea-blue sky, swifts scream.
A heavy lull across the valley.

An orange
　　　　drops
　　　　　　　one bee
　　　　　　　　　　roams the pots

Geranium, lupin, bougainvillea.

Tatay Nick's

The small tear in my faded, ex-German
postal workers jacket that snagged on
the nail
that held the string that held the lighter at
the door for single cigarette buyers
in Tatay Nick's sari-sari store
a week before our marriage.

I shovelled my palm into calamansi
like searching for the winning bingo ball,
two I stole to flavour the Ginebra
we might drink together that early morning.

His recipes passed on to grandchildren
his recipes massaged into their palms:
adobo, laing, ginataang libas
from leaves off the tree planted at the gate –
a seedling brought back from Bicol region
that now hues the loppy, tawny, dog
waiting to be walked.

On the living room rug he slept early,
curled into a question mark,
snoring through a western –
the stagecoach chased by arrows
on the flickering black and white screen
before the market run
in the dented Carter van.

Only his name above the store exists,
now they play mahjong on the green baize table
clacking into the night, sipping shorts.
In the yard's swelter his dogs sniff and yelp.

I couldn't leave without mentioning the cats.
The one that followed us in a procession
up to the sepulchre, that clammy afternoon.
Marmalade smudged, ribs like a rack of knives,
it sat beside us whilst we prayed.

Another at the wedding-do as we toasted
I felt a figure of eight
shift around my shins,
then at the last song it made itself seen.

Tatay is Tagalog for Father.
A sari-sari is a small shop based in the community that sells everyday general items.
Calamansi is a citrus hybrid predominantly cultivated in the Philippines.
Ginebra – a brand of gin made by Ginebra, San Miguel Inc.

Cosmonaut

Children dance and push
a council park roundabout
shaped like a flying saucer.
They spin it
try to make it take off,
a child trapped in a cyclone
white-knuckled on a whirling
hulk of metal.
They throw their weight behind, thrust
and shove,
a thousand laughing mouths
turning, turning
until he's Gagarin
orbiting the Earth.

The blur slows to a stop
to reveal a crew-cut boy
blinking
slashed in grease
strewn with space dust.
He slides off into a pile
seeing stars, he rises
walks drunk,
plaiting legs
falls.

I'm reminded of the babushka
with her offspring picking potatoes
carrying weight in an apron,
when a man falls from the sky
into the furrows of spuds.
Yuri dusted and shucked himself off
like a matryoshka doll.

The lad in the rec is upright,
he strolls forward
leaving herringbone trainer prints
his first baby steps on the moon.

Majorettes

It's the summer Springsteen is on fire,
they practice for hours on end in the park
for the Miner's gala,
twirling wands into 'X's like plane propellers.
The sound of nipsy players
whacking hickory sticks,
pommelling ovoid pottys into space.

A man carries a Christmas bag in May
clicking his tongue at the Jack Russell.
We stop off to natter to Mr. Bell
at the entrance of the nursing home,
to test him about football clubs and grounds.
Liver spots pattern his hands
like the underside of a dog's belly.
Roy and Dave pass by from coal picking,
pushing their donkey-bike laden with loot.

On their day,
Carol is angelic on glockenspiel,
against a palette of South Yorkshire grey.
Alison is run over with a lint roller.
She will march
behind a hoisted, red, colliery banner.
They will play 'Dancing in the Dark' on brass.
Ali flings her baton into the air
her open palms still waiting for the catch.

long day?*

murmurs a wall
as I lug
my shopping
home
well yes
house
what day is not
as we perch
on the edge
of extinction
please
keep
your solicitude
to yourself
except that
against my will
I feel myself responding
to wall's
random empathy
kindly brick voice
offering a bit of stony compassion
for a human hunching by
with her woes
on a fire-hot
end-of-the-world
summer's day

*graffiti on house wall
 in Kingswood Bristol

Prodigal

The Prodigal *Sleep* climbs into bed
with me at last

We sweep away god knows where
under the pastel quilt,

Napoleon
marching across Europe on the radio

As I slept
a longing came to me from long ago

I didn't know how to feel it
or whether it meant me harm

Nothing leaves its mark like longing

Even in sleep
there's no choice   no choosing

even the postman knows your name
and where you live

Longing raises itself
from the dead

looking just as lovely as it did
all those years ago

Longing's what you wake to
and what stays with you

hours after you've forgotten sleep
and all your powers therein

MARA BERGMAN

"We're Very Sorry for the Delay.
This Is Due to a Preceding Failed Train."

Two houses on the green hill
and a long wooden fence along the field.
Two horses – brown and browner –
the brown one facing away
from the browner one
lying on the grass in the sun,
a heap of sleep, all stillness
and heartbeat.

The leaves of bushes on the bank
along the track are nodding.
The wind is gentle.
The browner horse lifts its head
to reveal its shadow-head, and a shadow
under the brown horse appears,
a whole new horse. A magpie lands
on the grass. A white van passes
on the road in the distance.
Time stands still
so we can understand its movement.

Now the browner horse rises
and the two horses stand side by side,
then move closer till they are one –
horse, grass, sun, hill.
The one horse walks and walks
until the browner horse peels away
back towards the way we came
while the brown horse continues
in the direction we're going,
are hoping to go.

ROD WHITWORTH

Names, you know, names

It was Rod, the other one,
the one who listened to American radio
on his Communist dad's short wave,
who, one bright April morning
between the 53 bus stop and school, said
You've got to listen to this bloke,
a pianist, Thelonious Monk.
He's something else. Another world.
I told him no-one could be called
Thelonious Monk. It took me
two years to find out he was right,
on both counts. What he didn't know though
was that Monk's middle name was Sphere.
By the time I knew that,
the car Rod was travelling in
had crashed into the lamp post.

I am all the things I think I should be

I rise early and walk five miles
before a bowl of Greek yogurt,
strawberries, honey
made from my own bees.
My dahlias are blooming
so beautifully, aren't they?
And look! I baked a lemon drizzle!
But I won't have any,
not even a crumb, not even a lick
of the back of the knife.
I cook for my husband in a little apron,
a pastel blue that brings out my eyes.
Feta, potatoes, walnuts and mint,
in our south-facing garden,
one small glass of blush and my body
doesn't need the vitamin gummies,
quarter aspirin with my morning tea.
It just happens like it should, with no pain
and no bleeding, they just come
and I give them his name.

There's a Woman with a Baby in the Local Café

Peroxide hair, shaggy and cropped, effortless.
Tattoos of naked women up her arms.
She drinks her iced latte through a straw, laughs.
She looks tired but in a sexy way;
son gurgling away on her hip.
The kind of woman that has her own paintings
in her boldly painted living room,
a kitchen island, self-respect. I wish
I could say that I'm being poetic,
that this gorgeous woman is in fact
me, but there's moisturiser in my eye
and my flat is falling to bits.

Lambing season

As usual the cuts of meat hung cocked
in the butcher's window.
Elderly women came for their sausages.
Lambs hearts for the dogs. A new coffee shop
had opened up on the high street, serving
a shamelessly similar menu to the one
a few doors down. Never before had I felt
such an air of occasion.
The evenings were tinged periwinkle.
I was sober. Freckled. Loved.
Every so often I caught a slight whiff of petrol.
I didn't complain. How could I?
When the coffee was served with such flourish!
When I lost that first pregnancy it was so
deliciously warm. The sun beat down on the canal
like it had something to prove.
I drank it all. Pints of it. Tended to my garden.
Blocks of yellow butter. Children in Easter hats.

Titanic Sails into New York harbour

Disembarking, they wave away news
of an incident out there –
think what you will, ours is the story,
we are the only witnesses.

Later, in the bars, voices are quieter. Speaking of facts
I do remember something, one is saying.
The ship groaned.   Cabin lights flickered out.
People panicked, tried to steady their breathing.

Colossal jagged whitenesses slid past.
Nothing happened: a slight skirmish maybe.
I looked up at the brilliant spring stars. Somewhere else
there were shouts, cries, glass breaking, a klaxon.

Such calm, the familiar pulse-pulse,
God Himself among the stokers, great power-engines
working the deep, a soft pounding through those wastes
between us and the crowds where we are now.

Our unsinkable mythic city,
lights ablaze, out of the fog,
street by street passing beside us,
one step away into the same.

Nothing on Prime

after Tony Hoagland

I was trying to remember that film with a split-screen
storyline where two people's lives run parallel
and only the audience can see the full picture.

On one side the man is driving towards the site
of a bomb he knows is planted in a shopping mall.
On the other, his wife is running as fast as she can out of town.
She knows about the bomb but her car's been stolen.

As she belts round the corner, she smacks straight into
Denzel Washington, the guy she used to be in love with.
Without saying a word they start running together
and we can guess where this is going.

Meanwhile the husband, I forget who plays him,
has driven his car off the road – it's snowing now
and he's hurtling downhill through a forest
missing tree after tree by inches.

He's screaming the woman's name
as he comes to a stop, upside down,
hanging from his seatbelt. He's still trapped
while his wife checks into a motel with Denzel.

I needed to know if he got out, if she left him
for Denzel Washington. I needed to bring both halves
of the screen together. But I couldn't remember the name
of the film and there was nothing like it on Prime.

I fell asleep at eleven with the TV on mute.
I dreamt I was running through a field of poppies,
tripping over what I thought were stones
but turned out to be rusty helmets from World War I.

My feet were bandaged and bleeding.
From this I learned that you can't control what happens next.
Life is always split-screen with other lives running parallel.

St Christopher

It's late afternoon and we're seeking some shade.
St Christopher carrying Jesus on his shoulder stands by the door.

A silver sword hangs in a glass case behind the font, mysterious.
Today the three of us crossed the Derwent on stepping stones.

We formed a human chain, reaching back for each other.
It was the day the mayflies rose from the river, glittering.

City of Music

I'm standing on The Moor outside the new market.
The name's deceptive, there's nothing of a moor about it.

I can hear two buskers, one in each ear. The girl has a voice
that belongs on The Voice, the boy is struggling for top notes.

Then a third strikes up outside Boots. He's grizzled, playing
a confident saxophone solo over some American jazz band.

A woman next to me is leaning on the glass, vaping
as if her life depends on it and breathing out strawberries.

Buggies roll by, laden with carrier bags. The old
and the slow-moving shuffle in and out of the market hall.

Then suddenly, here come the wraiths,
moving improbably fast, focussed, speaking

a loud staccato language only they can understand.
Shoppers take a collective step back to let them pass.

Who'd have thought this done-up street with its polished
stone seats engraved with poetry would come to this?

The Thrush

That day in the library, a song thrush repeated
his best three tunes half a dozen times, as usual.
Then, after a pause, he switched to a newer set
of phrases. I noticed the change immediately
because there's a particular concentration, a particular
level of absorption about reading a book in a library.
I suppose that's why librarians object to noise.
The new notes sounded more like an alarm than
his previous joyful assertion of territory.
I can't explain the effect of the change of tone
but all the readers looked up from their books.
No-one moved. He sang again, urgent, insistent,
as if calling to us. Again and again he called.
One woman took a tissue from her bag and began to weep.

An Old New Yorker

The magazine flops open on the kitchen table.
The window admits the pinkish light.
"Is it ready?" the eldest calls. The fridge hums; if available,
the recipe on *Good Food* advises using *chervil*.
The chopping board is cleaned, the knife is out.
He'll wait a minute, turn the page to the cartoon.
There's a space where there should be a caption.

The chicken's a mess he subdivides,
a slippery, uneven pile-up that seems larger,
chopped, than it did 'whole'. He decides,
imagining the youngest on 'chervil', that omission's better,
and dices an onion, teary-eyed, while the news goes over
the same tune he'd left the house not quite singing
ten hours earlier with daylight coming:

Call the kids. Clear the table. Hurry up,
this shouldn't take years. A lifetime! Clean the counter.
Get the key, someone must go, for milk, to the shop.
Remind him about biscuits, says his sister,
following her brother. So they all round the corner.
Everything is cooking. He reads on from the back to the front,
head bent to a silence night has darkened.

Head bent to a silence night has darkened.
Everything is cooking. He reads on from the back to the front.
Following her brother, so they all round the corner,
"remind him about biscuits," says his sister.
Get the key. Someone must go, for milk, to the shop.
This shouldn't take *years*. A lifetime! Clean the counter.
Call the kids. Lay the table. Hurry *up*.

Agreeing what to hang

One year number 12 forked out
on multi-colour bunting to pre-empt the usual
red-white-and-blue; pure cotton
after mutterings of plastic rattling sleep.
Faded in weeks, and next year we dyed it
purple – Prince had died.
Then it was number 5's turn to buy: back to
red-white-and-blue – a royal wedding, or was it football, or
both? So I reckon folks just want a splash of flapping
colour and while I for one can't stand all that national crap,
community is compromise
and we'd never reach consensus
on pride-rainbows, skull-and-crossbones, anarchy, rags, black lace,
or number 7's wish, EU stars on blue,
so we let 5 go for it, only to find they'd misclicked and ordered
Union Jacks. Even they said oops.
But it's 12 who does the work each year and
with a triple extension ladder
and a frown like the carpenter nailing Christ to the cross
he hung it up.

10 was made up – can't you lot enjoy it? – while
7 was straight on the net getting flags-of-the-world in
polyester for next year, but for the duration and
despite objections behind closed doors and
those who didn't want their photo posted with it and
those who did want their photo posted with it
we lived with it and
kept our mouths shut.

Either

Jacqui sets this cool exercise to get us inventing stuff:
tell the class two facts about yourself,
one true, one made up – let them guess.

I say: I'm half German, half British, which is
why I was so hurt by Brexit, why I speak German
but didn't study it. My first name is personal,
mother tongue, spoken out shopping
but not round the base. Later, recalled here,
it got boxed up, spoken just on trips to Oma's by the Rhine,
stocking up on *Bravo* and cakes. We didn't talk about
Opa. My second name is patriarchal. It won the war.
Britain had Section 28; Germany, Paragraph 175.
I hold on to both passports.

I say: my mum and dad were both priests, shared a parish.
Both wore long black cassocks, stiff white collars.
Left to play in churchyards and vestries,
I grew up at the back end of religion.
Mum waited as the C of E trudged towards
equality, ordained first deaconess, then deacon,
then priest. Our house belonged to the church,
doubly; lunch was a staff meeting. Our phone rang
non-stop; it could be the funeral parlour, an engaged couple,
or a man I'd slept with.

Most of the class guess wrong.

Elves

No sooner have you said
you might as well believe
in an elf hidden in a muffin

than said elf
springs to mind,
revelling with fellow elves.

The Sadducees (old WYSIWYGs)
would have reviled
the very notion of elves

but we conceive a bevy
of elves, arch-elves and non-elves
in themselves

and relative
to the Ultimate Elf
presiding from its muffin.

Jack Fool

When I find he was a loner who loved
prayer and Minecraft; whose usernames included
TheExcaliburEffect; a Cyber Transport Systems
journeyman with TS/SCI clearance, who ran a
chatgroup called "Bear vs Pig" in
Discord's Thug Shaker Central;
that he surrendered impeccably to a SWAT team
outside his mother's home as helicopters hovered,
filming him in red shorts and T-shirt walking backwards,
hands-up; and that a man in the courtroom yelled
"Love you, Jack" to which he responded, "you too, Dad" –
and if I see myself as show-off, and set
aside those whose lives he jeopardised –
I can relate, I can.

Night Bombings

When the night bombings began
artificial suns tore open the sky
in flashes of such power — we waited
for our universe to explode.
There was no respite — the fears
of the day invaded our nights,
companions imposed upon us.
Amid the noise, the rattle of windows,
the counting of breath-pauses between
one detonation and the next —
we became night crawlers. Inhabitants
of dark spaces which wrapped tight
around our throats and would not let us breathe.

And on the ceiling, a lizard.

When he told her he had a little sister
the same age as her, she imagined
safety. A link. She braided
words into a chain of connection.

When he told her that his sister's
favourite subject was science
she lied and said – Mine too –
testing that bond of words.

When he stroked his moustache
and told her to lie down
When he rested his gun against the wall
and unbuckled his belt

she watched the dust motes hang silent
in the air and the lizard freeze
on the ceiling, and knew that words
had never had the power to save her.

Rananim

The garden gives way onto fields,
the fields, five of them, onto the sea,
the sky this morning a mottled grey,
the sea itself, indifferent,
flat as the eye can see.

When Lawrence lived here
he envisaged a community of writers,
a republic of letters bound by friendship.

In the meantime he made furniture,
planted a garden, grappled with
the final pages of 'Women in Love';
dashed Frieda's head against the wall
instead of his own.

We pull on our waterproofs
and walk up the lane;
flag down the bus into town,
wary of no more than rain.

Just sometimes, while you are sleeping,
I venture quietly downstairs,
run my fingers along a painted chest of drawers,
the back of a chair;
breathe in the shallow air.

Cornwall
Night

Driving back across the moor
a barn owl
caught for an instant
in the headlights

A shelf of cloud
black as anthracite
over the sea

The only sounds
the grumbling of my old heart;
your breathing
close in the cloistered dark.

PAULA CUNNINGHAM

Both

a line between the wild and settled regions/
the coloured band around heraldic shields
the seam/ rim/ edge/ periphery/ or frame or brink or margin/
a frontier//
a bed replete with herbiage or flowers
to put a border on or lie upon it/ to abut///

i laid myself upon it once
i made myself a crucifix
i laid myself along it/ upped and laid myself across//
i touched/ pressed/ rolled and tried myself against it/
the one snow falling hard on either side//
my open mouth was quickly filled/ ~~my purple lips encircled it~~
i whispered both inaudibly
and hummed the double-wonder

MARTIN REED

Apprentice

A slow clock oversaw the day
in our windowless shed of a musty workshop
where Syd and Tone talked people and pubs
I didn't know and cut up metal
with squawking shears, moulded it
round cylinders to shape and size

to make the pipes. My job, to wash
grease and dirt off every one,
from mighty tree-trunk basso profundo
that overhung each end of the bench,
all the way down to a piccolo
I could bathe in a bowl of soapy water.

Pipes corrode, breathe false notes,
taking the edge off Parry, Bach
and Mendelsohn; they can spoil the tunes
of snowy carols and bleating Easters,
christenings, marriages, funerals.
It made you think but we never did.

Syd, white apron and Stalin moustache,
answered *Eh!?* to every enquiry.
Tone never spoke a word to me.
We saw no leafy parishes,
just pencilled their names on the finished job:
New Milton, Thame, West Wycombe, Stroud.

No evensong chords vibrated our air
those hushed and endless afternoons;
no musical nave and chancel for us
or daffodil churchyard of ramshackle gravestones
where strains of *Down Ampney* harmonised
with the fleet, repeated song of a thrush.

Sake Bombs

I asked you for a light opposite
the painted ladies, who were not

statues of women, but houses. We
laughed at my mistake.

The man you were with you'd met
on the bus. He left. You were in

the business of friendship and took
me to your favourite spots, bought us

a pizza to share and a couple
of Sake bombs. We wandered in the sun

smoking your cigarettes two metres
from every door. You told me that

San Francisco is twinned with Bath
because both have seven hills; about

your jobs in London selling craft beers,
working in the V&A kitchen

with an oven from the 1600s; choosing
the dealers in clubs you managed

(taking home $125,000
per year from your cut). We left to play

pool and you showed me a picture
of your son practicing jiujitsu

and your ex-wife, mentioned the split,
told me about your ancestors'

immigration in the 1800s. We played
pinball. My friend picked me up

from outside the arcade
after finishing work. 'Who was that guy?'

they asked, driving away, you waving
at the car. I told them I had no idea.

The Woman

When she came into the deli, I was stood in my dirty navy apron
making baguettes for locals. Morris from the Market ordered ham,
cheese, lettuce, tomato, no cucumber. Butter. Homemade coleslaw.

Her coat was magnificent, like something a faerie would sew:
embroidered with gold and lime and rose and plum. The pattern
swirling and hypnotic, the fabric so soft. I told her I loved it.

She said, 'When I'm back, it's yours.' I waited years before I quit.

Whispering Bob

Her forty a day habit hadn't been slowed
by throat cancer and we called her
whispering Bob – her voice was like gravel
being slid off a flat-bed truck – I never
got to speak to her that much – and Jazbo
had a great idea – she'd nip to Heron's
and buy four or five packets of biscuits –
and we put a bowl by the staff room sink
and each time we ate a biccie or two
we chucked in five p – ten p – sometimes
a quid and the kitty for future biscuits swelled;
But we noticed the quids started to go missing-
Then the rest of the silver. We just wanted
a stash of biscuits and we could have …
given some money to Whispering Bob –
who clearly was desperate for it – but we didn't.

Smoking as a necessary thing

We all used to carry them, so if anyone said *have you*
got a light, we'd pull out our Bic lighters and the nearest
would oblige. No one ever asked for a cigarette unless
they lived on the street and we'd hand one over
and wish them well, because we had homes to go to,
and jobs that meant we had cigarettes in our pockets
or rucksacks or stashed in our bras. On Friday evenings,
when the winter sun had gone down early, we'd end up
in the bar on 78th, and I'd stand by the wall, so I could
lean on something, and smoke along with everyone else.
Sometimes I'd have an unlit cigarette between my lips,
my hand searching the recesses of my bag, when someone
would appear at my elbow, lighter clicking, so I could lean
into the flame. Sometimes the fire would linger after I'd lit up,
sometimes it was extinguished before I even inhaled, the curl
of smoke snaking down my body into my waiting lungs.
I still stand against walls, and remember the hand to mouth
motion, the flare of a match when the lighter ran out.

Diagnosis

If you notice my attention wanders   don't ask me
what's wrong   There are more books here than I can count
and I don't know where to start   Under the weathervane
the house is almost still   Eighteen months is a very long time
if you're trying to live each day   Five horses   five perfect horses
graze in the field out by Persac   two stand together   facing
opposite directions   shoulder to flank   This winter
the heating works in our car   we de-mist the windows
every morning in case the ambulance doesn't arrive   We must start
to find the letters to spell the words that will recast all this
back to how it was before last Wednesday

Full Moon

You call me out into the night air. I'm busy
making dinner but I put my slippers on
and emerge, grumbling. I've been inside all day,

a new habit, where I ignore the trees, the softened
air, the lighting-up of blossom on the apples,
the place I'm so grateful for. I'm wrapped up

in my hermit skin. I come out, *just for a moment*,
I say. *It's chilly*, I say, and move closer to you –
and you point up in the sky to a moon *that* big

and as bold and round as a poppy, pocked
with its own face, the eyes brighter than before,
and it balances there, as long as we want it to.

Don't get cold, I say, but now I lean into you,
and both your arms circle round me, and we
look up at this moon, this blood-orange moon,

our mouths open, the dinner waiting inside,
but we stand in the quiet, unmoving,
each moon granting us one more month.

Harry

I saw him in a café, and he looked pretty good, considering.
Downright handsome, in fact. Dishy. I wondered how he
had escaped, figured he must be over 90 by now and not
quite looking every inch of it. I sang him when I was 4 years
old, I told him, I sang him through my life. He looked
through me, which made sense. I heard him whispering,
lightly singing the opening lines to Jamaica Farewell – *down
the way where the nights are gay* – he looked around him – *and
the sun shines daily on the mountaintop* – and I opened my
mouth and I whispered the next line, and someone else – a
young woman breastfeeding a baby – took the next and the
office manager joined in and the waitstaff bounded out
from behind the bar in a conga and danced across the floor.
The guy with the face tattoo took up the next verse and we
were all there in that café singing – *but I'm sad to say, I'm on
my way, won't be back for many a day* – by which time we're all
weeping and whooping and laughing and crying at the same
time, as the flutes diminished and the guitar grew quiet and
in the room we all looked towards his table, where he had
sat, his coffee cup empty, his whispered voice everywhere.

The Conquistadores Encounter the Rain Forest

Tell us, O Mighty Don, O Don of the spreading foothills of the Pyrenees
O Don, whose forebears first pressed the grape for the blood-red wine
our pack-horses carry, tell us why we must enter this alien forest.

We seek El Dorado, compañeros, that we may return to Spain wealthy men.

Tell us, O Mighty Don, O Don of the great wide plains that stretch
from the vast Atlantic to the fish-dark Mediterranean,
tell us how we may find our way through this dense and darkened forest.

Ah compañeros, we shall follow the path the jaguar takes.

Tell us, O Don, the taker of pleasure from the wives of all Madrid,
O Mighty Don, whose seed has served a thousand mistresses,
tell us what will protect us from the perils and dangers of this forest.

We are armed with the arquebus, compañeros, and the musket.

Tell us, O Don, what are those creatures that swagger in the forest top
with eyes like the eyes of our long-dead ancestors,
and voices that roll like thunder at dawn and at dusk.

Those, compañeros, are howler monkeys, and their bite is neither fierce nor fatal.

And tell us, O Mighty Don, how you will keep us safe from the barbarians
whose shadows swarm before us and whose forest breath clings at our throats.

Compañeros, you do not need to fear: we bring them gifts which they cannot refuse.

Catherine

She's comfortable in her own
high-vis jacket. She's unapologetic.
Two consecutive nights now
I've dreamt myself

into her kitchen. Cuppa and a cig
out back with her and Clare.
I love Clare too, but Catherine
is my role model. From the

very beginning –
"I'm Catherine by the way…" –
to the huge, intense, quiet ending
Catherine Cawood is magnetic.

And when she's gone –
now she's gone – missed.
A Catherine-shaped hole
only Catherine can fill.

A bell on every tooth

I've got peas in my fridge older than you, she said,
and his head is full of slamming doors. Who
are you calling thicker than a Boxing Day shit?
Look at you in your matching shoes, you must
have had a hard paper-round. What did you come as?

The day felt back-endish, quiet as a bit of bread
could send a glass eye to sleep. So mean
it only breathed in. Yer arse in parsley, boy!
Like piffy on a rock-bun you are, so don't
piss down my back and tell me it's raining.

I never regret what I said, just where I said it.
They'd fight with their fingers, some people,
but you couldn't knock snow off the washing line –
go anywhere for a little apple, that one would,
not as green as she is cabbage-looking,

and all over me like a cheap suit, or a rash,
then on him just like a tramp on a kipper,
so hungry she could eat a buttered clog
or a scabby horse. Not my circus, not my monkey –
and hasn't been since Nazareth won the Cup.

It's fine having lead in your pencil, but you need
someone to write to. You had time to kill
a donkey with soft figs, you weren't run off your foot,
and you still don't know if you're punched, bored,
or countersunk, you grubby little tuppence.

Come here, or you'll go home lost, she added,
like your life. More holes than an Aero bar in that,
though it should be good, it cost enough. Get in,
soft lad, the cat's been out longer than you have. It's not
the end of the world, but you can see it from there.

The Ghost Walks

That evening I stood astride the mid-road line
one minute, two, soaking in the hush. Clear
a mile each way it was, clear as lanes entangling
the distant Minster it stretched to, where ghost-walks
had gone from streets that were ghosts of themselves –
though choked now with ghosts more than ever
in Stonegate, Piccadilly, Pavement, everywhere
unapparent on our screens, thickening sick air
where it slid invisible, pronged, aghast. Daft
with abandonment a few still took selfies
defiant down snickelways; but fog, as in some
crazed newreel, was congealing. No bombs
would fall there, but the masked cortèges filed by
to curt interments. Pasts curdled unpeopled
presents, phantasmal, briefed with lies. Just days
before, beneath the walls, we noted the hostel
from which its spilth had issued, the index case.
By the blue plaque to Snow of York, who blocked
off Soho's cholera-well, by the station-yard
where bubonic plague-pits groaned, by the Ouse
you could now hear susurrant, a dissolution
in which dead selves might rise unappeased
supped at the blood-trench dailiness once filled,
immersed in mortmain hurts all had hoped
long solved, like trains being chartered to run on
that still ran on empty, bright windows bodiless,
like the dying teen Skyping home one final time
still saying *Don't cry, Mum, I'll make you proud*.
Should that make us angry? Sad? My brother says:
It was just like someone was standing on my chest,
as I halt to rest against the doorpost of Margaret
Clitherow always struggling for her last breath.

The shocking thing is

'I can say EVERYTHING if it can be smuggled
inside something else.'
– Tara Bergin, The Fabulist

The shocking thing is
how well the lions are fed

The shocking thing is
the ponies appear content

The shocking thing is
the dogs whimper to play football

The shocking thing is
the lions comply with the act

The shocking thing is
laundry, laundry, socks

The shocking thing is
I walk through that door every day

The shocking thing is
gear drying near the fire

The shocking thing is
the contortionist shut in a box

The shocking thing is
elephants on each other's backs

The shocking thing is
I pace from the sink to the door

The shocking thing is
the weight that each seal heaves

The shocking thing is
I pace from the yard to the sink

The shocking thing is
the bears have been known to attack

The shocking thing is
all our costumes are frayed

The shocking thing is
the lions have to stay

Circus and no children

Imagine! Instead, ponies
trotting alongside me,
nuzzling without question.

Soft noses against my skirt.
Wild eyes calm and unseeking.
Just an apple for intimacy. Strong

as I am. Supple and capable
of bearing a throne if needed.
A pony is up and away within hours

galloping beside the mare.
Each pony grows taller daily
but never taller than its mother.

Everyone knows the circus
was invented by a horseman
back from the war with dashing

feats of agility and escape. Before
that, the chariots raced potently
round and around. What a whirl

I thought the circus was
when I was a girl. And now
I can't bear to think of the stands

empty of my children.
But I could command
a pony to follow me.

The lion tamer's funeral

Not a carnival but a plague.

The lions didn't attend,
the audience wasn't permitted
to view him this once.

He was buried without
hat or whip: what was in the box
was all that could fit.

The body of his body
was suited in his latest jacket,
crisply lined with green:

his ex-wife and daughter
saw to that. You could almost
believe them still married,
the way she carried on.

Here was a magic box
with no trick.

DAVID UNDERDOWN

Two species at the aquarium

Plate glass, twenty-mill., this is their event horizon: to one side these,
myriad, scarlet, vertebrate, taking a cue from their surroundings;
to the other a single biped, human – one year old.

Back-lit, with feet on terra firma, her fingers splay against the radiance.
She is a library of unfilled shelves, eyes wide to this close encounter.
The shoal, like clustered comets in deep space, is inches from her face.

Across the gulf their differences: they, bounded tight by the tonnage of water;
she, earthbound, breathing air. On either side, the troposphere they share
upheld by frail light eight minutes from its sun.

AZIZ DIXON

For Lydia

I am remembering you in Bernwood.
I have not forgotten you are in my sling
sleeping where you can hear
my heartbeat, while I

orienteer a route through trees
as if I were not yet a parent,
triangulate off a path junction,
one a road less travelled

and if I had not met your mother
that day on Alnmouth beach,
sat next to her on the minibus
you would not be here with me

walking above your new home
where four cuckoos are courting,
flying up the valley
telegraph pole by telegraph pole

and you are learning Welsh
from the children in forest school
who are your family
for now.

Notes on intimacy

- I knew you would be good for me
- When I set your toiletry basket on fire
- And you were quietly alarmed
- But helped me extinguish it
- Said it was a bit of excitement for the evening
- We used the same melted basket
- For another year

Notes on Commuting

- I drive over the M1 at 7.28am
- The speed has been reduced to 40
- Above we are crawling too
- I turn up the volume
- My eyes are on the road
- But now I'm on a pastel pink bicycle
- I am cycling through summer in Paris
- Carla Bruni is singing
- *Que de nos chagrins il s'en fait des manteaux*
- I am complicated, mid-twenties with long brown hair
- Maybe Sally Rooney is my mother
- I stop to look over the Seine
- Pick a cherry from my basket
- Tease the pip with my teeth
- Spit it into the river
- Carla and Paris fade

The First Week

At first I was pretending
to be a mother; the baby
confused, adrift on the bed

and nothing passing us
all day – just the ice cream van
parking up quietly.

But we kept introducing
ourselves – strangers at the
threshold of motherhood

where nothing's forgotten,
and nothing's remembered,
the warnings, the wishes,

the bad advice, the mist falling
on the way to the hospital
careless and improbable.

Real

The robot birds were jealous of the real birds. They had less in common than they'd been given to believe. Nest-building for example, was a mystery. Whatever material the robot birds gathered, however carefully they placed one fragment on top of another, their nests wouldn't hold.

One spring the robots bullied the birds out of the garden and stole their nests. Within weeks they had crumbled to nothing and couldn't be repaired. Without the birds around to measure themselves against, the robots felt even more unbirdlike.

The children that played beneath their trees were a consolation; as delighted by the robots as they ever were by the birds. But the adults seemed dissatisfied, until eventually they mislaid even the memory of their loss.

Come Home

be small again in front of the fire
before the red stars blazing

at the end of the world, before
the old forests burning

MARILYN LONGSTAFF

Goo goo g'joob

Le Massina bar, Rond-point De Gaulle, Plouharnel Friday Market

The egg man isn't here today.
Maybe his hens aren't laying.
Last week, he drove his van

into the pavement parasols,
oblivious of we old hippies
lapping up September sun.

The bloody traffic's here though
on this main route to Quiberon:
huge lorries of every kind,

multitudes of campervans, and
surfers, off to the Côte Sauvage
pour Le Weekend. The convoy

of Bikers, all the same, all
desperate to be different,
younger. Over fifty years,

we reminisce, since John sang
I am the walrus, admire
the ancient cyclist, posing

in Piet Mondrian windcheater
and vibrant yellow baseball cap.
Not dead yet. No, not dead yet.

SARAH MNATZAGANIAN

It's all written

on a piece of paper, folded into a simple boat.
I take it, light as it seems, to the Ouse and crouch
in the reeds, let the boat feel water start to soak the keel

as the wind takes it, that spidery scrawl still climbing
the bilges, calling back *I haven't finished with you yet*.

The boat and its reflection shrink into the mirror
of distance. A coot calls out in alarm and a fish
makes a circle on the ceiling of its world.

Words sail past willows, past cows knee deep
and drooling, lifting tails and shitting into the current.

It's over. There's no time for regret when kingfishers
rainbow the afternoon, a bittern booms
and swifts fight over the last few flies.

The boat will sink past Cuckoo Bridge, its black ink
re-written into watercolour by the river: purple,
yellow, blue words I'll never write again.

Victoria Avenue, Newtownards

The side wall of the Young Farmer's Club is the place to tell it
how [   ] is the biggest heroin dealer in the area
how [   ] is nothing but a dirty tout
then there's [   ] the slut and homewrecker

how [   ] is the biggest heroin dealer in the area
this wall is the best place in town for that bulletin
then there's [   ] the slut and homewrecker
if all else fails write the person you hate mistreats children

this wall is the best place in town for that bulletin
to say what you want to say about the police
if all else fails write the person you hate mistreats children
spray paint about the state of the government – it's a release

to say what you want to say about the police
at the weekend a young farmer with a paint roller will blot it out
spray paint about the state of the government – it's a release
come Monday the canvas will be primed for you to shout

at the weekend a young farmer with a paint roller will blot it out
the side wall of the Young Farmer's Club is the place to tell it
come Monday the canvas will be primed for you to shout
magnolia rectangle to name them and keep your own name hid

And I ask why can't I be happy to be comfortable?

The basins, the damp-catchers, the towels rolled up, the sliding roof that let the rain in. Whole winters saturated. Every room I wrote at that time came leaking, pages sodden. Not so long ago, either. When a friend says, 'For a woman to have it all she has to do it all and not ask for help', I hear, 'She has to *do it all*'. Why would a woman work unless she's getting paid? What might people say if she just scraped by? I won a diamond at the casino. I mean, I bought a diamond with the money I won at the casino, had it set in a band. I prised that stone from white gold teeth. Needing cash, I took it to a jeweller. Wiped my tears with the cheque. Threw the thin gasping ring in a drawer. The cut was marquise. I liked naming things. Impractical, it plucked everything anyway. Child, I worry it would have scarred your cheek. They called a woman 'cheap' for forgetting to eat during a flight. For not taking the opportunity when it presented: a smiling cabin crew member appearing by her side with a cart and a question. Not an offer. Not a giveaway. I can recall where the empties are in muscle memory. I recall it all in a far-fetched, otherworldly part of me. I sold on baby furniture telling myself a baby needs so little. I changed you on my knee. More babies came and more money went. But that was then and now is now, which can also become then, and then, and then again.

When I woke first on the way back from France

Perhaps I died on that coach, sitting beside my long-lost, red-haired sister.
Thirty years ago, my face buried in rabbit fur. Nose stuffed. Gasping for breath.
I released the bunny I used as comfort and cushion; Claire had one matching.
Her in a sleuthless sleep, and all around, dark.

Everyone sat like spools, eyes shut. Just me and the dash's needles moving.
The back of an empty driver's seat. The cooling, lamplit English lanes.
The newspaper too carefully positioned on one wilted teacher's lap?
Front-page headline screaming of a school coach crash horror.

Perhaps this is how I'd know. Because what was the point
in a bright tunnel calling? Death was smarter than that; I wasn't.
I needed it spelt out while a faceless something moved us on.
And, you know, it was all right; I felt serene until someone woke
and suddenly there I was: Alone, alive and wrong.

The Blue Bridge

A truss bridge, to be technical; in Knight's Park, the
sauciest part of Kingston, at its patchwork confluence
with Surbiton.
The chords of either arch
present a tempting post-pub dare:
inches narrow;
double-decker height
above the chalkstream shallows
of the Hogsmill's grunt towards Old Father Thames's
indifferent embrace.
My friend Paloma insists on this:
that after the brutal aggro at the Sham 69 gig,
she watched her boiler-suited Kinetic Sculpture lecturer
pigeon-step halfway, stumble–tumble
and land midriver
on the platform heels
of his steel-toecap boots.

49

Self-portrait, Mauritshuis

I've come for the Rembrandt. He's on a wall by himself,
his right cheek reddish; he is 52, after all. He's wearing
a flat, black beret. You can smell the drink on him.
As I move closer, I hear his breath, slightly wheezy.
If he stood in my place now, he'd be mightily pleased
with the effect of the white splodge in his eye.
If he stood here now, people would crowd round him
for a selfie. He'd be polite, then gruff, want to take
a closer look at the Vermeer opposite, the young
woman with wineglass, laughing at the man
with the hat we can only see from behind.

You missed the last bus

Because you were standing on the wrong side of the road
and only that because someone had stolen your bike
and only that because someone else had driven through
red lights and left you with a write-off and only that

Because you'd walked-out of a job that paid the bills
but punished you when you failed to persuade people
to settle their accounts and that only on account of your
father who too had started too late, left too early.

Short enough to submit to Pome

Throughout the summer evenings of persistent drizzle
we sat under canvas, chewing tobacco.
Such evenings are a gift. Songs will come.
Smoke in your eyes and a clock
on a folding teak table.

Coastal Path

Firstly, my phone charger: plugged in beside the kettle
in the kitchen of the flat we rented in Holyhead
before the first day's walking. A home of hearts
and affirmations on cushions, the pair of us
around the firepit, staring at stars. The charger
forgotten in the flurry of setting out.

Next, my reading glasses: left, perhaps, on the beach
at Porth Trefadog, where we collapsed to rest our feet –
or dropped somewhere between there and Cable Bay
after anxious checking of the map, though when I tracked
back the miles between gorse and fence, on sand, grass
and shingle, I still couldn't find them.

Thirdly, my purse, scattered with my belongings over the floor
of the welcoming loft with Velux windows opening
to the sea and delicious breakfast brought to our door
wrapped in a blanket; it matched the pattern on the rug
and I didn't notice. The bracken that day was the colour
of burnt honeycomb and curlews were piping.

Today, with time stretched across the sky, we are walking
quietly, often apart, enjoying our rhythms of heart and feet,
reassured by signs which come thoughtfully placed.
Now and then, we wait for each other, on new ground,
holding so many threads of other walks: some we still
hope to do, and many we thought we'd lost.

An invitation to sit in the sun

You painted it ash grey, placed it at the bottom
of the garden, where no-one sat on it. No-one
wants to be seen not knowing quite what to do.

Last week we brought it back to the patio,
took care to stand it sturdy so the cobbles
wouldn't wobble coffee cups, unnerving guests.

I watch it while I wash up, waiting for rain
to dry from it, cats to nap on it, ivy to curl
through it. I imagine myself observing

my homelife from outside, deciding whether
to escape into a book or keep on staring in,
piercing the gauze of what we think we've become.

Blues

i.m. Dennis Casling

Since Dennis thinks the world's gone home he sings
to plates and benches, table legs and walls.
He croons each phrase so round and long it rings
the air's soft bell back and forth. He calls
and bevelled glass provides. Breaks off to test
a note dissolve in silence, then cranks the blues
to scale this hall's big sound: its sweet unrest
some debt to pleasure, self paying his dues.

You move. You want to soft-shoe through the song
leave lines intact, but Dennis hears you rub
against the boom and still keeps on: what's one
rogue punter ghosting through his smoky club
no sooner here than out the swinging door.
He serenades the last man in the room
his sponsor, pal, his backing from the floor
who holds and in return belts back the tune.

Mistake

She stops you, hand on arm. *How are you, Paul?*
You disappoint, you're someone else, a fake.
These frames, you say, this buzz-cut-grey, happens all
the time. When strangers shout at their mistake
from cars, or swear they've stood you beers in bars
beside which ocean? You've been police, a nurse
a thief: callings so wide you wear the scars
of dumb surprise. You'd just confuse them. Or worse.

But you are Paul she states, as if on cue.
This tale you've floated lands no weight or shape
and she wants to draft the narrative of you –
so why bang on and spoil a clean escape:
sure, you're Paul. *Oh man* she says*, I miss
his presence still.* You catch this dark-sweet scent
pooled about her throat as she comes to kiss
her ghost, his bristled cheek, wherever you went.

The Brontë Holdings

Dear Nell ▮ /
I speak to my sister as night follows
day. I speak to her when I have nothing
to say. She is in when God isn't
but she isn't God and must grow tired
of my voice with its threadbare want.
Papa will have no summer dresses – no light
curtains in the house. *My striped dress
is not cut crossways*, it falls
in a peculiar way. I lose myself
rearranging its stripes, worrying
at threads. The hours drag on
for hours. Sometimes the hours drag on
for days. You will forgive this foolish
letter.
Dear Nell –

Anna Woodford and **Tara Bergin** have been collaborating on a project with the working title 'The Thunder Residency', making poems in response to archival holdings at the Brontë Museum at Haworth. The poem 'Dear Nell' is part of a sequence that responds to letters by Charlotte Brontë. The project is ongoing.

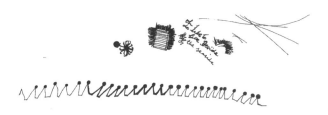

Dear Nell / *my striped dress
is*

one small sheet /
folded into four leaves /
all leaves used /
pinholes in top of all leaves /
paper /
ink

I pin Faith on your reply.

My mother wants to put a bomb under the house

That's what she yells from her perch on the ladder
as she empties the airing cupboard of sheets that won't fit
and shredded towels that float like moulted feathers.

Her six children scatter, it's not safe to hang around.
I hide in the bathroom and keep the door locked,
I don't want to be there for what happens next.

So that's where I'll stop it, mid-explosion
suspended like an installation in a gallery
and I watch as the filaments spread through the air.

Until all the washing surfaces in my memory,
draped over the piano and hung from the stairs,
steam rising as it airs and exhales like our sins.

My mother on a bicycle

Almost awake she picks up speed
to cycle over O'Connell Bridge –
nothing stops the small surprising girl
who fixes a puncture faster than her brothers.
She'll reach Sandymount before she wakes,
she'll see the sea, stand on the cliffs.

Every night she dreams the same dream;
it runs like the blade of a knife tested
across her skin until the cut is made
when she wakes to traffic on the Hagley Road,
November rain on copper beech and tarmac.
Then my mother knows where she is.

Five a.m. she'll get up to sweep and mop
to be back before the children wake.
And how could I know all this? I still have
a tiny puncture kit into which everything fits.

How my mother made a fruitcake

There is of course no recipe
only the memory of my mother
unsteady on chairs and countertops
reaching into cupboards for spice
and flour to add to the dark fruits
and jewels of candied peel and cherries
my father bought at the cash-and-carry
or Tesco at Five Ways, his favourite shop.
He'd start it off, then she'd take over
and beat the butter and sugar to ominous
incantations about her oven 'playing up'.
Each year the same uncertainty and now
I can taste the memory but there is no recipe.

Come Early

Yesterday you asked what tree we're having.
I asked what you meant and you said *it's December 22nd,*
we usually have the tree up by now.

This morning I'm out for a walk while you sleep in.
Hot cross buns and chocolate eggs are eaten,
daffodils are crisping, grape hyacinth is shy under a hedge.

Grey wagtails are pairing, rooks carry nesting materials
in their beaks. The first fierce shoots of Himalayan Balsam
break the soil, rowan trees are coming into bud.
An early dog rose swirls her bright skirts in the wind.

And the clouds are pewter.
And all the dogs I meet are black.

55

Gelt

53.4306°N 2.0025°W

'Three coiners are ordered be drawn on a sledge to the place
of execution.'
Leeds Intelligencer, 10 April 1775

It begins in a hidden clough. Empty bellies,
piecework lacking, the oats failing,
mothers' milk drying. Too many mouths.
Hartley learns a new trade, a way to spin
gold from dross. The shuttles fall still

across the valley, in Bell House, White Lee,
Keelham, Burnt Acres, Stannery End.
At Barbary's inn, in Mytholmroyd, the gelt
gets passed under her tables, from delver
to spinner to 'prentice alchemist.

By rushy light, with dogs on watch
they clip and file and gather slivers
finer than frost on a yew berry, breath
held, roughened fingers fumbling
like bridegrooms at the prize.

The smelt gold bubbles and pours
into moulds and sets, a hundred
flaring moorland suns, their light
hidden by thick mossed walls.
Tongues are tied by fear and threat.

Tom Sunderland, painter, becomes
engraver, narrows the swagger of his hand
to a fine acquaintance with pistoles,
and moidores which in these days swim
unremarked among our pounds and pence.

Hartley, crowned King David, reigns
in all of Calder, these cloughs which thrive
and fatten, reap the crop. But trust
and silence melt like snow in summer.
Excisemen, ambush, lieutenants, trials.

The Tyburn tree at Knavesmire,
the *three-legged mare*, sprouts
a royal rider; its short drop stifles
all his kingly proclamations.
He is a man again, clipped back.

To my sons, about secrets

after Mila Haugová

I can't tell you anything about the afternoon
I stood at my sister's front door, admiring her garden—

the blue delphiniums and the silvery
fuzz of lamb's ears that crowded the brick path.

I can't tell you how long I waited for her to swing
the door open, her daughter held to her hip

gumming a rusk and wearing the velvet hat
I had given for her birthday. My sister invited me inside

but I can't tell you anything about that. We drank tea—
Earl Grey from bone china dressed in rosebuds.

We sat on her floral lounge, sunlight pouring in
through clean windows, the child unsteady

around the coffee table. I can't tell you what we ate.
Perhaps it was her famous apple cake, thick

with cinnamon crumb, or my mother's scones
complete with clotted cream. I can tell you I was thinking

of nothing in particular when she placed her cup
precisely back in the saucer and cleared her throat.

That's when I noticed more flowerbeds outside, the riot
of orange hollyhocks, the open mouths of the snapdragons.

I can't tell you what she told me about our father
when I knocked my cup, tipped my tea so it pooled

on the carpet in a large brown stain. She told me not to tell.

Ali and the Lamb

Ali lived on a farm with a little lamb that followed her everywhere. The lamb head-butted people she didn't like. One time we all went to a barn dance, riding shotgun in her dad's truck. Everyone sat on hay bales and drank lager from plastic cups. There was weird dancing like line dancing or something. We poured lager into a bowl. The lamb drank and drank until its eyes went big as saucers and its legs got wobbly. And later Ali came to see the baby at the flat with her boyfriend who I think beat her cos she always had bruises up her arms. They brought M&S party food, garlic balls and chocolate cheesecake and pink fizz and we played old Led Zep records and got pretty drunk. Ali must have seen the baby before because she came to my wedding – that cold day in April and everyone dressed like they were at a funeral and the lamb already gone to slaughter.

Shadow Bear

We've lost the word they used to have for bear.
That word we have is just the shadow word
they used instead, lumbering from thickets

of old germanic texts: *bera, bruin, björn,*
meaning 'brown one'. With that word we roll
a whispered fear around our mouths, an age-old

trick of keeping fate at bay, hear unspoken magic
in lost names. Gouges on a tree. Tracks from the forest
through the snow. Sometime in the night a shadow

passed this way. *Bera, bruin, björn,* the one
drawn to the fire or cooking pot, trailing a feral smell
of death in teeth and claw and fur. It is the same

with most things we bear. We say 'they passed',
are 'no longer with us', 'gone'. Refuse to call it cancer
on a scan, as though this might stop lengthening

shadows merging into night, ward off a heavy pad
of nearing footsteps, fill the silence when they stop
to sniff the air outside your door.

The Great Aunts

Every summer there'd be an afternoon
of visiting, sitting in front rooms
where windows rarely opened,
being asked to stand up straight
to see how much we'd grown.
Warned not to touch the Scottie dog
or china ballerinas dancing
between the various knick-knacks
on their crowded mantle-shelves.
They'd fan tea cakes, pink wafers,
wagon wheels on paper doilies,
pretend not to hear mum saying
that's enough now to offer us another.
When it was time to go, they'd rummage
in handbags smelling of butterscotch
for pocket money, kisses on our cheeks
damp as lemon sponge. Sometimes Dad
would drive them to Shorehead for tea,
where they'd pick at fish and chips,
before devouring ice-cream sundaes
topped with glacé cherries, rainbow sprinkles.
The talk of poor Harry, Andrew, Dave –
even now I'm not sure who was married
to whose brother, which ones were simply
nana's friends. These bird-like women,
hips held in place by pins, who just craved
a little sugar at the end, their desserts
in fancy glasses, eaten with long spoons.

Self-Portrait

Maybe Picasso, with both eyes askew
and everything else equally weird.
Or blocks of colour courtesy of Rothko,
red for the unexpressed passion,
white for the blankness of unfilled pages.
And black. Black for the deep places.

No, think of me as a Jackson Pollock.
A mess. Madness created by a bicycle tyre
which matches my wrinkles and loose skin,
eyes whose bags have their own dark bags
of weariness, trying to fight like
a gladiator without a sword.

And then there's the art of children
which maybe captures me most.
I'm a bus with the four wheels on one side,
A square house with smoke rising
from a wobbly chimney.
The stick woman who needs a stick.

Kyoto

Cherry blossom is more
than important to the Japanese.

When and where it appears
is broadcast on radio, tv and social media.

After a day, it has disappeared
completely. It seems

there are a mere few minutes
when it's perfect and in full bloom.

Before and after this birth and death,
just as when you walk a Japanese garden,

you trace the short line
of life from beginning to end.

Like in the brief haiku, mystery is packed
into every fleeting petal.

That year we saw avenues of bloom.
This year I see barren trees.

At My Table

sparrows fluttering a flock
of chestnut wings come flying in
the din of them chirruping
to and fro the wall the hedge
incidental notes to my life
the chatter pulls me out of myself
waiting for the right moment
they knock each other off impatient
I know there is enough
heaven in all this chitter
wings beating strong the clamour
deafening I worry it will end
my flock of intimates close to the house
it rains so hard I cannot stand it
a step away from winter

Middleton

The drive over Sutton Moor is fixed in me:
skies huge and weighty, all that glistening,
emerald grassland, the bird's eye views
above Cowling village, a merlin diving,
farmland steeply sloping, dipping down
the field of horses where the car slows.
Amble up the track to Wolf Stones, Nan Scar,
these are the things that come back to me,
the Pennine Way,

                    not the one street hamlet
close to meadows, the gate that creaks
not the front garden, no, not the boy
whose name confounds me, who never spoke,
the last supper in the kitchen made of wood,
not the bed, sacrificial, bang in the middle
of the room, the patchwork quilt softly fraying
not that you didn't ask me to stay.

Stocktake

My Science teacher took stock of us,
in the Autumn of 1998.
Some of you will leave he said,
some of you will have babies
before you finish here,
some of you won't pass the exams
and at least one of you will die.

He looked like Jasper Carrott
and I took it all as a joke.
Wrote the title, wrote the date,
waited for the real lesson.

Emma was pregnant when
we did our exams, hid it only
by vomiting before arriving at school,
and the girl who sat chanting *tea leaf* over her technology paper
was escorted from the room as a distraction.
I showed up slightly drunk,
waited for the hall to take their seats so that I could find mine,
didn't care much for testing,
didn't test myself much at all.

No one died until school just ended.
Spring 2003, hit by a car on his way to nowhere very important.
I remember the road being closed
and walking the back way to the
shopping centre, my friend and I sat on a wall
absorbing the break in traffic.
Things moved slowly.
I took moments for noticing, yet
didn't know then what had happened.

The whole school was invited to
the funeral and young people stood
outside the church, crying for each other
and what they thought was sadness
and I was somewhat cold and said
it would be unfair for me to grieve
a person I didn't mourn.

But even now
I turn my head from time to time,
see his face in a picture in my mind;
aged 11 when we shared a form room
and a table because our surnames
shared space in the alphabet.
I think of him practising for a life
he never lived, the school hallways
and the waiting.
He played football and was thin,
and he sat there the same as I did when
our teacher said we'd die –
and I wonder if he laughed, like I did,
or – wrote his name and the date,
underlined it like a headstone
in the Spring.

Vespers

They set to sea, the three of them, without
So much as a bean between them, *God will watch us*
And when we've sufficiently fasted, He'll provide.
Monks had a madness then. It made them do things
Crazy for faith and always come back safe
And wiser home.
                                One of the monks, the youngest,
Back then when they set out
Not much more than a boy, his chin just fuzzing
(He lived a century, is now a saint), declared
I will take the little cat as a companion.
So they put to sea, and pointed out beyond
The last peninsula, the furthest-hurled island of their archipelago
Until there were only waves. They said the psalms
Over and over, then slept, and when they woke
The currach had snagged on a rock and the four horizons
Showed no land at all. They said their psalms
Again and slept again and when they woke
This time a giant salmon lay full length between them.
The little cat washed her face,
She scratched up under her chin, she watched
Them and the enormous fish.
They inspected her paws, they were just cat paws,
Cat claws, small and cushioned, dry, and her fur
Dry too, she hadn't been in the sea at all, just mist
Made her a little damp. No sign of the hand
Of God, and yet there was no denying the huge fish
Was some kind of counter evidence.
They slept again and when they woke this time
On the rock that held them fast embers were cooling:
The salmon quite cooked, impatient to be eaten.
The cat washed her little paws and smoothed her dark whiskers.
They ate, they gave a sliver of fish to the cat

And sang the psalms once more, then ate again
And sang until they were full of faith and salmon.

They sailed back home, praising the good Lord God.
The little cat sat at the bow and kept watch
For the first land bird and the chimney of their hovel,
The little tower in which the bell that counted time
Lived and called them. There it was, it was chiming Vespers.
They would land as the mist was shaping, in time for prayer.

Pillion

The servant girl spreads the laundered cliches
Out on the sunny ledge to let them dry.
Made unfamiliar without a stem or a source
They shimmer like peculiar leaves and petals.
She is singing the kind of song a servant girl
Sings when she's undisturbed and merry enough
Because 'it's almost Sunday', wondering
Will the weather hold, will he be there at the gate
On his red Vespa, revving to carry her off,
Hugging him round the chest, holding the hot
Smell of him and the engine and they're gone.
Is he thinking about her, too, how he will
Hold her, fold her, unfold, will he be waiting?
She sings her sort of song. I hear from the terrace
Where I read, in the shade, the same page over and over
Or is the ever altering poet (Ovid)
Ringing, ringing, ringing, ringing the same changes.

Stripping a dry-stone wall

As if an air-lock has breathed itself open
or a shepherd boy's broken the cave's clay seal
the wall's cracked heart comes out.

The divided dark is drier than you'd know
(thread-roots grow – old ladies' whiskers)
as if its dust could only imagine
quiet skies or sunlight stroking the heather.

Like a pedal-bin, the dead hands that built it
chucked stuff in: look, the soft cow-tongue of
a boot, and here, wire-rimmed glasses
fold neat as a blackbird's bones. Then today,
I swear, an ink-pot, brown and cold as stone.

I brought it home and now up from the black
a tiny face I don't know stares back.

A Week after her Heart Stops, My Mother-in-law turns up Unannounced

No no no no no, she drifts between
my temples, a faint smell of cigarettes.

You couldn't have shown up a little sooner?
I ask, wondering why she'd let

her poor neighbour follow that smell
all the way to its source.

She fogs behind my eyes, wailing
from her miscalculated abyss.

We could have helped you, I lie, knowing
I'd accept she was tired

when she passed out watching the kids.
Her slurred speech, a side effect

of her dietary supplements.
I'd hear the percussion of pills

in her handbag and tell myself
it was a silver rattle

for the new grandchild
she was so excited to meet.

Alaska has the Highest Reported Rape Crime in America

We didn't know this when we vacationed there
off-grid, during Christmas, without a rental car.
If we did, would we have still sucked the length
of our candy canes and given our address
to that guy on the flight to Fairbanks? Laughed
at his jokes and made him promise to come
get us a week later from our cabin, chauffeur
us back to the airport? Would we have still
been the kind of girls who walked out of
baggage claim into a snowstorm, thumbs
outstretched? Hitched a ride with that Alaskan
who put a bullet between the eyes of a grizzly,
and then, when a cub emerged from the bush
to paw at its mother, killed that too?
Would his tyre chains still sound like sleigh bells
as he drove us miles from a phone signal?
Would we still see the terrain we passed
through as picturesque had we known
a serial killer released women into that wild
and hunted them like caribou?
Would we still think the state flower beautiful
if we knew about all the dead women?
Forget-me-not. Forgotten. Petals blued
like our bodies, side by side, on ice.

Fridge
(after Thomas Lux)

You're quite new, stainless steel,
smears on the doors, easy to see,
easy to wipe away. It's almost a pleasure
to unload the perishables, to feed you,
or let you settle with our worldly salad leaves,
mushrooms and margarine.

Fridge, you are a showroom for those 'shrooms.
Each shelf is a floor that we visit
with our eyes and with our hands.
Your salad drawer is a salon.
Spring onions refuse to turn into slime.
Tomatoes stay spectacular,
and I have plans to sauté the life
out of those thin green beans.

You are a taken-for-granted fridge.
Never flashing your temperature when you get too hot.
Never freezing the milk when you're not.
You never alarm me at all, except,
when your door is left open for too long.

Then you beep like a chemo drip
when the bag's empty, or the delivery of poison
from the cannula, for whatever reason,
has stopped.

Some plants that grow on a tree won't fall out of the tree

A gift of a morning –
each path, a lucky path.

Everything vies for attention –
on the slope that leads to Goody Bridge,
or, if you turn left, up Silver Howe.

You stop to look at baby ferns.
growing on the trunk of a tree,
turn, look back, and back again,
at Helm Crag, down, at the white house
and the sky is as blue as you would wish it,
only 9am and set to be like this all day.

You test yourself.
The first few feet, over rocks,
how far would you, could you, go on your own?
Today, not far at all in your head,
you'd take as long as it took
to climb Silver Howe.

It's the coming down that's more worrying.
Ideally, you'd have sticks to balance –
Norwegian Walking Poles,
retractable, easily tucked away,
to take the pressure off.

Time enough to think it through.

Two women, where two paths cross,
are looking at a map. It's early.
For now, you have your bearings.

HELEN ANGELL

I Just Called To Say

There are no 'ordinary' days and I think
you know that, Mr Wonder. Even on a winter
lockdown morning, folding my pyjamas
and resting them on the toilet seat, fingers

brailing the bobbled tartan. The choice
of one shampoo over another changes
the course of the day and at breakfast
the chopping board blushes with the blood

of Spanish strawberries. Their insides white
and hard, unlike the robin visiting daily
in a fuss of sparrows to pom-pom the arch
of dead bramble I haven't cut back. It's legal

at least, to sit with other people in our gardens
now and we will, although the sky is as grey
as all the paints mixed in a palette, mardy
no matter how much white or yellow you add.

SAFIA KHAN

There is this smell

in the downstairs hallway. A thick foul cloud, smothering the
air like rotten sage. I open windows, check the gas, sell by dates.
Go for a walk while it clings to my body, heavy as wet cotton.
Message the neighbour *can you smell that??* She replies *omg
we thought it was just us*. Parents paste fliers on lampposts in
concerned colours. Local nuisance metastasises into international
uproar. Panic blooms like a new bruise. Election campaigns
run on odour reform. Closed access journals report correlation
between socioeconomic status and scent
burden. Entrepreneurs court investors with a data-driven
approach to global-scale eradication. (They are later arrested on
fraud charges.) The neighbour shares a link to her boyfriend's
livestream. He blames the foreigners then thanks today's sponsor.
We carry on holding our noses.

Sitting on a rooftop

The clouds crouch as they dispense rain.
Crows leap from the ridge tiles.
Children walking home from school

dance and laugh as a cyclist wobbles.
A delivery man walks backwards
carrying a container of fish, ice-cream

and coq au vin.
The builder next door sits on a roof
smokes, drinks coffee and watches it all.

Georgiopolis

warm water
calm sea
it s the day to try
I swim parallel
to the shore
enjoy the water

I grow tired
put my foot down
nothing to hold me
try to calm myself
breathe
swim towards the shore

I test the depth
splash gurgle
head under
Janine grabs me
I've got you mum

All at once on a Wednesday afternoon

I have the remains of lunch with me   aubergine curry in cardboard bowl
     I am in the belly of the library   my book isn't on the reservation shelf
my phone rings and it is the surgeon   who rejigged the nerve in my arm
     I get another call from the ultrasound   people I finally have a slot
it is early for dinner but I can't stop   eating the warm clumps of rice
     the woman is helpful finds my book   A Winter Book on the shelves
can I get back to you I ask the surgeon   I am in a library it is loud
     the ultrasound people tell me to fast   for six hours bloat myself with water
I asked to keep the end of my curry   arranged in my backpack like a hammock
     the book has a snowy cover blueish   calm but the library is always hot
I tell the surgeon it is still sore when I lean   on it he says more baby oil
     I tell my mother   about the ultrasound I haven't had to fast for one before
I am in the library and I am all belly   full of water the promise or threat of it
     I am a waxy hunk of scar on an elbow   in a scratchy jumper on a warm day
here is a book from Finland from the snowy past   she found it saved it for me
     I have more curry left to eat   it hasn't spilt yet hasn't collapsed in on itself.

BLIND CRITICISM

In this feature we ask two writers to respond to a poem without knowing the author. For this issue we're delighted to say that **Serena Alagappan** and **Em Pritchard** took up the challenge. Author and poem details are given on inside back cover

Safety Behaviour

The thoughts, I'd been told, to put somewhere else.
So I put them on the roof. I put them in a box
and post them. I put them in shoes I never wear.
I split them up from each other and put each
               one inside
a stranger's pocket, to be taken home and washed so
the thoughts drown in several different washing
               machines.
I put them on the wing of an aeroplane. Inside
               a hollow
bit of wall. I tie them to balloons and they fly off.
I put them in the ocean and they swim away. I hold
them over a candle and they evaporate. I hide,
no, bake them, inside an enormous, delicious cake,
seven tiers high, and I give a piece of it to everyone.

SERENA ALAGAPPAN

Safety behaviours are enacted in an effort to prevent fears from coming true. For instance, if you are worried about being called on, you might sit in the back of a classroom to avoid being noticed by the teacher. The poem 'Safety Behviour' engages the psychological concept in the singular as opposed to the plural – reinforcing this patterned action as amorphous. As many of us know, when anxiety is amorphous, it is all the more difficult to tame.

So too are the 'thoughts' in this poem, difficult to tame. Because the speaker of the poem has been told to put them 'somewhere else', the lyric confesses 'I put them on the roof' 'in a box' 'on the wing of an aeroplane'. What follows is a litany of hiding spots: 'a stranger's pocket' 'a hollow bit of wall' 'in shoes I never wear'. The poet successfully defamiliarises ordinary locations as containers for dread.

The thoughts also acquire agency: they 'fly off' 'swim away' and 'evaporate'. The author's choice to grammatically animate the thoughts has metaphorical implications. When one catastrophizes – perceives a situation considerably worse than it is, or presumes a terrible outcome before it has occurred – anxiety leads the charge. The poet ironically offers the 'thoughts' (which are notably not presented with the epithet 'anxious' or 'intrusive') an active role in the speaker's attempted diversion of them. This choice feels mimetic of real life. Don't we all avoid confronting these types of 'thoughts'? How much control do they have over us? How much havoc can they wreak?

There are layers to the concealment and

The author's choice to grammatically animate the thoughts has metaphorical implications.

compartmentalization of the thoughts in the poem. The poem follows the speaker literally trying to 'box' them, and though a line break interrupts the action, the speaker wants to get even further away: 'I put them in a box / and post them.'

The insistence of the speaker to 'put' the thoughts 'somewhere', seems, by poem's end, like a desperation to put them *anywhere*. In the final line, the poet teases a redemptive gesture – the thoughts are now couched somewhere 'delicious' – a 'cake, / seven tiers high'. This false ending preempts the ultimate deliverance of the lyric. Have the thoughts then been whipped into sub-mission, cloyed by batter, and leavened into something sweet and light? Is the cake reserved for the baker?

No, the speaker admits: 'I give a piece of it to everyone.'

EM PRITCHARD

This poem takes a casual metaphor – the age-old advice of 'putting' your thoughts 'somewhere else' – and runs with it, exploring the difficulties and absurdity of such advice. Although it is clear that the poem is about anxious, possibly obsessive thoughts ('Safety Behaviour' refers to attempts to stop fears coming true, in the context of anxiety disorders), none of the thoughts themselves are divulged to the reader. This choice might suggest that the thoughts are unspeakable, too terrible to acknowledge, but also leaves room for the reader to project their own anxious fixations into the poem.

The pervasive anxiety that runs through the poem begins with the jarring commas of the opening sentence. The instruction is uncomfortable, ill-fitting to the problem it purports to be solving. From the second line on, however, the poem gets into a rhythm, the long list of actions showing just how many thoughts there are that need to be discarded. Putting these thoughts somewhere else feels like a full-time job, and the form of the poem adds to this. In its compressed sonnet-like shape, the poem feels heavy, blocky, with

no room to breathe in between different thoughts. To me, the domestic images, such as the candle and the shoes, work better than the bigger images like the plane and the ocean. It is easier to imagine someone actually trying to enact these things, in desperation; in these lines, the metaphor feels most closely tied to the frustration it describes.

The ending of the poem is ambiguous. It all depends on how we read the self-correction of 'I hide, / no, bake them': is the speaker really wanting to move away from hiding their thoughts, towards being more open? Part of me wants to read it this way, as a successful transformation of the thoughts into something palatable, digestible, that can be shared (a trouble shared is a trouble halved!) But a larger part of me reads the ending as troubling. The change from 'hide' to 'bake' can also read as an elision in itself, hiding the idea of hiding. This implies that there is shame and suspicion involved, that the thoughts continue to exist, inside other people: transformed into something tasty, but not gone. For some reason I think of this ending as a much darker version of Wendy Cope's 'The Orange' – the huge orange becoming a huge cake (a tier for each day of the week), and rather than being given to named and known individuals, it is given to 'everyone', an anxious fantasy of the feeding of the five thousand.

The pervasive anxiety that runs through the poem begins with the jarring commas of the opening sentence.

About the Authors

Serena Alagapan is a winner of the New Poets Prize and features on p74 of this issue.

Em Pritchard is a poet, critic and bookseller – also a member of the Writing Squad and a (check it out) digital Poet in Residence at the Poetry Business.

New POETS PRIZE

JUDGED BY KIM MOORE

SUPPORTED BY ARVON AND ARTS COUNCIL ENGLAND

CALEB LEOW for his collection, *Human Waste*;

FREYA BANTIFF for her collection, *All Appears Ordinary*;

IMOGEN WADE for her collection, *Fire Safety*;

LUKE WORTHY for his collection, *On What Could Sting*.

Imogen and Luke will take up an Arvon residential course of their choice and Caleb and Freya will have pamphlets published in March 2024 under the New Poets List – an imprint of The Poetry Business. All four winners will appear in *The North 70* (winter, 2023).

See pages 74 –81 for poems from the collections of the 2022 winners, Serena Alagappan, Tom Branfoot, Beth Davies, and Chloe Elliott.

CALEB LEOW
for Human Waste

A pamphlet which interrogates human waste is a risky strategy – but in these wide-ranging, inventive poems, it absolutely pays off. The objectification of the body – whether that is the migrant body, the female body or the working class body is held up to the light through skilful handling of form and imagery. – Kim Moore

Caleb Leow is an emerging poet from Singapore. He won third place in the inaugural Oxford Poetry Prize (2022) and his poems have been recognised in the Bridport Prize and the National Poetry Competition. He studies History and French at the University of Oxford.

FREYA BANTIFF
for All Appears Ordinary

Nothing is truly ordinary in this extraordinary pamphlet, where owls are 'light as an eyelash blown for luck' and where illness and pain can be rinsed and washed away like stains. These poems keep the faith that language can illuminate anything – from everyday acts of love like the removal of nits from a child's head to the extinction of a species. – Kim Moore

Freya Bantiff is a Sheffield poet. She was placed third in the National Poetry Competition last year and was highly commended in the Ginkgo Prize. She has also won the Bridport Poetry Prize (18-25s) and the Walter Swan Poetry Prize (also for 18-25s). Freya's poems and stories have been placed in the Aesthetica Creative Writing Award, and the Mslexia Flash Fiction Competition. She is completing an MA in Poetry at UEA and will take on the role of Apprentice Poet in Residence at Ilkley Literature Festival in October 2023..

IMOGEN WADE
for Fire Safety

There's a wild and magical energy at work in these evocative, sensual poems. Desire and violence, safety and danger, hunger and satiation co-exist uneasily in the same landscape, where the Green Man can wink from the ceiling of a church, and the world itself can seize you by the shoulders. – Kim Moore

Imogen Wade has been commended for the Foyle Young Poets of the Year Award, the Plough Poetry Prize and the Winchester Poetry Festival Prize. Her work also has been acknowledged by the Wells Festival of Literature Poetry Competition, the AUB International Poetry Prize, the Ware Poets and Frosted Fire Press. She has been published in *The Poetry Review*. After studying English at the University of Exeter and Vassar College, she trained as a counsellor at the Cornwall Counselling Institute.

LUKE WORTHY
for On What Could Sting

From a jellyfish like a 'tumour of salt and sand' to a meditation on Putin's penis and toxic masculinity – these poems are full of surprising images and wide-ranging in their interrogations – of class, sexuality, homophobia and masculinity. – Kim Moore

Luke Worthy is a queer poet and fiction writer from Sheffield. His work has been published, or is forthcoming, in journals and anthologies including *Poetry Wales*, *fourteen poems*, Broken Sleep's *Masculinity: An Anthology of Modern Voices* (2024), *Youth Word Up* (2017/2018), *Surfing the Twilight* (2019) and *Dear Life* (2022). In 2023 he was highly commended in the E.H.P Barnard Poetry Prize and was Young Poet-in-Residence at Sheaf Poetry Festival. Luke was commissioned to write a piece of children's literature for Leeds 2023 and is a member of Hive Poetry Collective.

WINNER OF THE 2022 NEW POETS PRIZE

Pamphlet | 9781914914478 | £6
eBook | 9781914914485 | £4.50
June 2023

*S*ensitive to Temperature seeks out the precariousness and sensitivities of language, as well as the fragilities of the world it represents. These are eco-poems that experience time on a human and non-human scale, from the movements of rock to the sources of rivers.

These poems feel as if they move in and out of consciousness, preoccupied with the language of psychology, tapered by wonder and restraint. There's a casual knowingness to the work which encourages the reader to also peer beyond their reality, in the hope something new appears.

– Anthony Anaxagorou

Serena Alagappan received her A.B. in comparative literature and creative writing from Princeton University. She then studied social anthropology and literature at Oxford as a Rhodes Scholar. She has edited poetry for the thirtieth annual Mays Anthology and the Oxford Review of Books. Her poems have appeared in The London Magazine, The American Journal of Poetry, the Colorado Review, and elsewhere. .

SERENA ALAGAPPAN

even now, assembling

even now, this dreamscape is assembling,
even as the screws twist left. the only
thing we built together is unfinished:

the dresser's cardboard spine pinned, but drawers on
the floor, severed panels I step over
in the dark. noting each detail, I watched

you count each nail. because I'm impatient,
I'll leave it this way—gaping—with sunrise
seeping through my window shades. I want to

wake with a stutter or a slap. I no
longer believe in things coming ready-
made. I expect to need a hammer. when I've

slept enough, I'll pluck a costume off its
hanger, and when I spin in that pretty
dress, it'll be like screws are in my feet.

slipface

gazing up at a long shallow angle of loose sand recalls
the typical dread: *if I reach out, will you make*
time for me?

the steep lee size of those aeolian landforms involves erosion:
what is left besides deflation, desert, and pavement?

there exist geological agents, such as rivers, glaciers, and waves, water—
really—who offer sediment. among these transformations comes

has the moment passed? sun radiates off the slipface, and longing in its breath, I
shake my head toward the dune. no, I say. *the moment's*
never passed with you.

Let's Catch Up Soon

You'd like to ventriloquize
that leaf, or the veins bulging
inside it, cul-de-sac
of the clementine wedge,
bumpy with seeds (one more
dead end street). Pulp thick
with fruit hair, tree blood,
lavender honey, syrup
boiled and tapped, one more
sweet thing to extract.

Waiting for fruits to soften
is waiting for a friend
with whom it's been a long
time since you've spoken.

You'd like to ventriloquize
the rot, the fur, the bowl going
bad, the brown parts of the
peach, the mush of berries, apple
skin wrinkling, pieces of flesh re-
consumed by soil. It's true,
you speak for muck, but time
is still mould: hold
your breath, (deceptive
cadence), it grows.

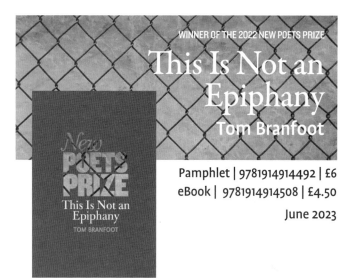

WINNER OF THE 2022 NEW POETS PRIZE

This Is Not an Epiphany
Tom Branfoot

Pamphlet | 9781914914492 | £6
eBook | 9781914914508 | £4.50

June 2023

Tom Branfoot's *This is Not an Epiphany* examines inner and outer landscapes that have become inhospitable; where people are 'burnt / by business as usual'. This collection is attentive to shifting landscapes where warehouses spring up on empty land, and the incremental austerities that constitute our living; its lyric absorbs the shocks and crises of survival within them.

These are formal, intelligent poems demonstrating an immense control of language and lineation. At their core is a restlessness, a searching presented as a series of inwards questions which never quite find their resolve. They keep going until the question itself becomes the endgame.

– Anthony Anaxagorou

Tom Branfoot is the writer-in-residence at Manchester Cathedral and a recipient of the New Poets Prize 2022. He organises the poetry reading series More Song in Bradford.

TOM BRANFOOT

Return Thursday, 14th

slant cities pass in a sentence
I am fed up   with all this reaching
for an approximation of beauty

was it not the brutish hour
the lights knocked out   like teeth
I am no one to speak

now   in the darker half of the year
bleed me like a radiator   at the station
because the world is big

take these hands   because the earth
is bending to a point
bleed me like a sacrifice   outside

light fades   in a page
The demand for love writes Barthes
in his autobiography suspended in white

sharp and tied   to no subordinate clause
this   is the stuff that lingers
in the stubbed October night

and I still text in longing
as if anything that came out of language
could make language tremble

Lodgings

if you knew it would happen then why
did you let it   *on my tod* meaning
death meaning ivy meaning own
rows of poplars in a lawned
golf course do nothing   the hedge
fund managers do nothing
knowing property is the square root of rain
if you knew entropy   would you reproduce
or that green on maps wasn't accessible
would you even move
I am a carpark crowded with carsized aches
an old elevator with wrought
iron doors creaking with the weight
of my civil disobedience   bladder
like a cloud   fuck this I want a house
in the country pebbledashed with stars

Portrait of a Garden

nuzzled in the crook
of your grinding teeth
I think the poem a terrarium
embracing an air plant
outside   plum blossom
bunch on trees
planted in avenues
this sticky garden
cultivated   in a single
bed hanging in a city
uninhabitable
money leaking through
the roof when it rains
some form of water
torture   discordant
with hedgerow choir
this rented room
sclera-white   daylight
pinching at the blinds
already I'm thinking
about standing
desk exercises   fibre bars
and waiting a whole
long day to arrive   back
under the damp ceiling
cracked   by heatwave
and your light feet
tracing patterns
in plaster dust

WINNER OF THE 2022 NEW POETS PRIZE

The Pretence of Understanding

Beth Davies

Pamphlet | 9781914914515 | £6
eBook | 9781914914522 | £4.50
June 2023

The Pretence of Understanding explores loss, not just of loved ones but of youth and adolescence. In these poems where time can stand still or run backwards, the reader finds themselves caught in longing moments of looking back at childhood; they remind us to run in the snow while we get the chance.

A beautifully strange and encoded book. I was particularly drawn to the tensions made between a place and a self – the longing to connect while remaining cautious as to what that connection asked for.

— Anthony Anaxagorou

Beth Davies (she/her) is an emerging poet based in Sheffield. Her poetry has been published in *Poetry Wales*, *Atrium*, *Rust + Moth*, and *Pulp Poets Press*, as well as in anthologies such as Candlestick Press' *Ten Poems about Flowers* and Valley Press' *Verse Matters*. She won second place in the 2021 Dead Cat Poetry Prize and in the 2022 Magdalena Young Poets Prize. In addition to being a member of Hive Poetry Collective, Beth is a graduate of The Writing Squad, Durham University Slam Team, and Sheffield Young Writers.

BETH DAVIES

The Wonderful Everyday

What strangers live here? I look around the living room
for clues. Maybe he's the music lover and it's his record player
on the side table, brand new but missing the needle.

She loves to read her favourite book over and over,
but buys a new copy each time (the same edition),
hoping for a different ending. Identical books

crowd the shelves. He doesn't mind because the spines
match the wallpaper. The drawing on the fridge shows
a triangle-roofed house, a row of faceless stick figures

waving in the front garden – parental love evident
from the act of display. I wonder whether they are happy,
wearing their stock smiles in a wedding photo, teeth

impossibly bright. In the kitchen cupboard, I find jars filled
with pictures of food. They sustain themselves
on the ideas of things. Is this enough to build a life from?

Are these three walls enough? Maybe they are saving up
for a fourth. Looking up, I see the ceiling is much further away
than it should be – enough empty air to call *sky*.

Is that where they've gone, the family who lived here?
I imagine following them up the half-made stairs
onto an upper floor that doesn't exist.

Scene

Tonight, they are shouting again
in the gardens behind my house.
The performance drifts over the hedge,
through an open window,

into my kitchen, its voices too distant
for me to follow the plot. I only make out
snatches: a shouted name,
an exclamation of surprise, a scream –

hints of stories unfolding just beyond
the edges of my life. Even without
audible words, the cadence of comedy
is distinct from that of tragedy.

I hear the laughter but not the joke.
Perhaps it is enough that people nearby
are happy. Perhaps I do not need
to know why. When the play ends,

I suppress my instinct
to join in with the applause.

Floriography

Like me, they were afraid
of how words bloom between
people. They preferred the silence
of a bouquet left on a doorstep or a heart
worn in a buttonhole. They understood

what I don't: the significance
of a carnation's shade, the melancholy
of a red geranium in a left hand,
how orange lilies know as much of hatred
as fists do, the bittersweet of nightshade

and truth. Is there a flower
for the feelings that have taken root
in my chest? If I pressed petals
between these pages, would you know
what I am trying to say?

WINNER OF THE 2022 NEW POETS PRIZE

Encyclopaedia
Chloe Elliott

Pamphlet | 9781914914539 | £6
eBook | 9781914914546 | £4.50
June 2023

Chloe Elliott's *Encyclopaedia* is playful and visceral, exploring boundaries of identity and the search for meaning in poems that delight with richly tactile language. Formally varied, these poems are unflinching in their physicality.

A well balanced mix of pastiche and observation; Elliott's worlds fixate on the idiosyncratic, surreal and absurd. Each associative turn seems loaded with news, humour, crisis or intrigue.

– Anthony Anaxagorou

Chloe Elliott is a poet based in York. She is the Gold Winner of the 2020 Creative Future Writers' Award. Her writing has featured in *Poetry Birmingham Literary Journal*, *bath magg*, *Strix*, *The North*, *Bedtime Stories for the End of the World* and *Magma*, amongst others. She is currently Creative Apprentice for *Modern Poetry in Translation* and works for *Aesthetica*.

CHLOE ELLIOTT

Dreamtheory

I am fearing my own coldness, I mean the parts
of myself that are resolute, are hovering inside
of me like plasma. Derrida says infinite alterity,
the completely other, the dead, living in us.
Like issues of chia seed. Ghostly cell walls,
translucent to the point of purple, a fraction
I cannot cross. I can't begin again.
I'm so sick of newness. Give me the beehive,
the piecebag, the quilt. I carry you with me
wherever I go.

Cow

After Blast Beach and the Tarot of Marseilles

III

We go searching for the cows, for their black
belted bodies. We find the Empress in the field,
woman of no longing. White ribbon splices open
her turnball coat like a harpoon through a whale.
I am a daughter of doubt, don't believe Tommy
when he says the sea is over there, make no notice
of the blue that degrades into larger, deeper blue.
But it does, farmers scythe the land, bodies grow
in mildew, we shuffle the cards.

XIV

Dragonfly wings butter in the sun
like smoked herring. The slickness of the day
catches at an angel's halo. It's hot enough
to persuade the angel to slip out of her wings,
those two halves of an auburn heart matted
like a pheasant. She slips out of her deck
and leads us to a red bridge over a coastal train track.
Uses shells to make crucifixions at the bits in her legs
she hates, carving out skin like spouts of a strawberry planter.
The coves stretch out like great labyrinths,
their slick bellies baking in salt and algae.
Belts of seaweed scream like the mangled pipes
of a choral organ. She doesn't make a big deal
out of it but she's got a choice to make.

X

Tommy's telling me how as a child his father would
get him to carry beechwood. Broad flat planks curved
like a muscle, kind enough to be stacked into dens
or barbecue grills. His father once dived into a rockpool
fully clothed to fetch him out. Dropped out of art college
and made all the National Trust designs, stole engines, dealt
cranberry glass and then stopped for the good pots and sweet babies.
Tommy cooks too many mushrooms and his coats always
smell of weed but he's got an angel on his chest and
a dove on his shoulder. Soft hands and dark brown eyes
like a boy I once knew in Tuscany. I'd give him the Priest,
the Lovers, the Wheel. I'd give him a field of terracotta statues,
eyeholes cinched with pencils. I'd give every smack
and sunny blunt of the Apollo and then a heart that matched.
An orange satin dress wet in the rain. I'd walk into the waves
and fish him out with the whelk and the worst parts of ourselves.
There's so many things I'm hiding behind. But the sea was there
the whole time – the hard tortoiseshells in their pelts telling
                us to choose,
the backs of belted Galloways like two right-winged angels,
the great heaving strapped to the sky.

We are delighted to announce the winners of

THE 2023 INTERNATIONAL BOOK & PAMPHLET Competition

Congratulations to
the winners as chosen by
Hannah Lowe

Doreen Gurrey for her collection, *A Coalition of Cheetahs* and **Laurie Bolger** for her collection, *Lady*

Congratulations also to **Mary Allen**, **Clementine E. Burnley**, **Lauren O'Donovan**, **Lydia Harris**, **Ramona Herdman**, and **Michael Greavy** whose respective collections were Highly Commended by the judges.

Judges comments

I was delighted by the pamphlets submitted for this year's Book and Pamphlet Competition. The standard of work was very high, and it was tough to choose from such attentive and humane collections. As always, poetry continues to reflect our social and political times, and amongst these collections is fine writing about the body, gender, working and family histories, migration and diaspora.

    – Hannah Lowe

The two winning collections will be launched in 2024 at Wordsworth, Grasmere and published 1st February 2024. 'Poems by the two winners and six highly commended poets will feature in issue 70 of *The North* magazine, which is out this Winter.

See pages 86 – 93 for poems from the collections of the 2022 winners, Karen Downs-Barton, Jon Miller, Zoë Walkington, and Luke Samuel Yates

Book & Pamphlet Competition Winners

Doreen Gurrey
for her collection *A Coalition of Cheetahs*

Doreen Gurrey trained as an English and drama teacher and for several years ran her own Youth Theatre Company. She went on to become an Adult Literacy Tutor writing and delivering Family Learning courses for the local council. Latterly she has worked as a Creative Writing tutor at York University. Her work has appeared in *Poetry Salzburg Review, The North* and *The Yorkshire Anthology*. She has won prizes in The McClellan, Bridport and Troubadour poetry competitions. Doreen lives in York and has five grown up children.

Varied in subject matter, these poems are clearly in the control of a singular voice. There is wonderful use of imagery throughout and surprising metaphor in abundance, in gentle and inventive poems that explores ideas of love, home, family and loss.

– Hannah Lowe

Laurie Bolger
for her collection *Lady*

Laurie Bolger is a London based writer and founder of The Creative Writing Breakfast Club. Her work has featured at Glastonbury, TATE, RA & Sky Arts & has appeared in *The Poetry Review, The London Magazine, Moth, Magma, Crannog, Stand,* & *Trinity College Icarus*. Laurie's writing has been shortlisted for The Bridport Prize, Live Canon, Winchester & Sylvia Plath Prizes. Her poem 'Parkland Walk' was awarded first place in The 2022 Moth Poetry Prize. Laurie's latest work explores autonomy, love & her working class Irish heritage. "Dazzling, moving, witty and insightful poems which look at the world with an oft-surreal eye, and show the lives, the truths, the people, who might ordinarily be overlooked." (Andrew McMillan)

These poems of memory and girlhood are powerful evocations of the changing body and the male gaze. A raw, absurdist humour provides a sense of defiance throughout, and the tone is in turns sad, angry, rue.

– Hannah Lowe

Book & Pamphlet Competition Highly Commended

Mary Allen

I have spent my life in the arts. Initially I was an actor (rep, Rocky Horror Show, Godspell). Then, after many years as an arts management consultant, I became a chief executive, of Watermans Arts Centre, Arts Council England and The Royal Opera House. Subsequently I was an executive coach and joined several boards, including New Writing South of which I was chair. I have been writing poems for about ten years, but have sent very few out. This is my first ever submission to a competition.

Lauren O'Donovan

Lauren O'Donovan is a writer from Cork, Ireland. In 2023, she won the Cúirt New Writing Prize in Poetry and was also short-listed for Listowel Writers' Week Collection Award and the Fish Poetry Prize. In 2022, Lauren was awarded Arts Council funding to work towards her first collection along with a Munster Literature Centre Mentorship. She has published work in journals and anthologies such as: *Rattle Magazine, Southword, Skylight 47, The Galway Review, The Galway Advertiser, The Honest Ulsterman, A New Ulster, Cork Words, Augur Magazine, Green Ink, Grand Little Things, The Quarryman*, and *Swerve*.

Ramona Herdman

Ramona Herdman's recent publications are *Glut* (Nine Arches Press), *A warm and snouting thing* (The Emma Press) and *Bottle* (Happen*Stance* Press). *Glut* was one of *The Telegraph*'s '20 best poetry books of 2022 to buy for Christmas'. Ramona lives in Norwich and is a committee member for Café Writers.

Clementine E. Burnley

Born in Cameroon, Clementine E. Burnley now lives and works between the UK and Germany. Clementine has an MSc in Applied Linguistics from Manchester University. She is currently a part-time, practice-based student at the Research Society for Process Oriented Psychotherapy where she studies conflict facilitation. Clementine has been published in *Ink, Sweat & Tears, Magma*, and *The Poetry Review*. In 2022 she was the RSL Sky Award Winner for creative nonfiction. As well as writing poetry she's working on a nonfiction book about her family history.

Lydia Harris

Lydia Harris has made her home in the Orkney island of Westray. Her first pamphlet *Glad Not to be the Corpse* was published by Smiths Knoll in 2012. In 2017 she held a Scottish Book Trust New Writer's Award. Her first full collection *Objects for Private Devotion* published by Pindrop was long listed for the Highland Book Prize.

Michael Greavy

Michael Greavy is a teacher from Manchester living on the edge of West Yorkshire. He has written and performed poetry at Edinburgh, Ilkley and Manchester festivals. Recent poems published in *The North, Magma, Stand, Acumen* and *The Frogmore Papers*. His work has been long-listed for the Bridport Prize.

We're delighted that work by these chosen writers will be featured in *East of The North* as well as the next print issue of the magazine.

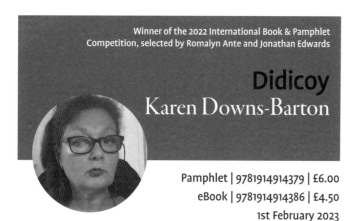

Winner of the 2022 International Book & Pamphlet Competition, selected by Romalyn Ante and Jonathan Edwards

Didicoy
Karen Downs-Barton

Pamphlet | 9781914914379 | £6.00
eBook | 9781914914386 | £4.50
1st February 2023

*D*idicoy offers a window into the colourful, precarious world of a multiracial Romany family, and focuses on characters at the often untold margins of society. Blending lyricism with formal experimentation, these poems explore what it is to belong. Clear-eyed and outspoken, *Didicoy* has something of the impact of a contemporary *Cathy Come Home*.

The ability to take subject matter of great importance and express it through significant formal gifts makes the impact of these poems breathtaking. Writing like this, which combines real expressive skill with material which must *be expressed, really reminds us what poetry is for.*

– Jonathan Edwards

Karen Downs-Barton is an award-winning Anglo-Romani writer. After a peripatetic early life including times in state child-care she is now based in Wiltshire. Karen is a PhD candidate at Kings College London writing a magic realist poetry collection set in a metropolitan revue bar. Her work has been widely anthologised and appeared in magazines including *Tears in the Fence*; *The High Window*; *Rattle*; *Ink, Sweat and Tears*; and *The North* amongst others.

KAREN DOWNS-BARTON

Of the Men who Came as Shadows in the Night

i

I didn't tell you
that I remember
splinters
of your father
his charry skin   fingers
with nails of polished wood
his Calypsos and dark beauty
how on Palace Road
I played with his children

I did not say I remember him
as a form brewing
beyond stained glass   his threats
or entreaties while he taught our door
to buck against its hinges
his unhinged kicking   shouldering   lasting and lasting
before disappearing
into the black silence
of his lost battles

why conjecture about his
imploded world
the wife and sons who left him
or the role our mother played   you
growing inside her
but I told you
that you were wanted
that's the thing
you should remember

Mageripen: The Rules of Hygiene

i.

In state children's homes, clothes you arrived in
are taken away for washing and you
might never see them again. The prefects
collect clothes in plastic baskets, ovals
big enough to take a ride in, skidded
across the linoleum landing. Boys
force each other's sweaty heads into piles
of knickers, scolded by laughing nurses.
New children who ask after their own clothes
are teased with tales of gifts to jumble sales,
burnings in boilers. But if you are sent
to the caretaker's office he'll let you
watch machines churn clothes in greyed water, spot
your waving jumper and kicking trousers.

ii

Your waving jumper and kicking trousers
decorate bushes far from each other.
A windy wash day beside Nans *vardo*.
You learn what a *Romani chai* should know:
separate clothes by body parts, top half
in white bowls, bottom half in blue, sprinkle
fistfuls of snowflake soap, swirl water to
blizzards. Scrub, wring, rinse, wring. This *mokerdi*
lore shapes rituals of cleaning. Nan's bowls are
emptied according to function. Cleaner
water near kitchen shrubs where fennel, mint
or lavender are gathered, bottom half
water is slushed in ditches, raw hands washed
to touch the bunched clothes, cleaned of their grey swill.

iii

To touch the bunched clothes, washed in their grey swill,
the caretaker uses callipers, hoiks
steamy meshed arms, legs, bodies to tumble
dry. Mist sighs from a drooping proboscis
hanging at a part-opened window. Fust
lingers on clothing, skin. I imagine him
as a dung beetle with pincer mandibles
rolling shit-ball clothes. Under the motto
Personal Possessions Breed Discontent
I practise the pretence of interest
in the wonders of his washing machines.
I'm looking for the clothing I arrived in.
It won't be stealing. No one here wants
to wear clothes worn by a 'dirty Gypsy'.

Winner of the 2022 International Book & Pamphlet Competition, selected by Romalyn Ante and Jonathan Edwards

Past Tense Future Imperfect

Jon Miller

Pamphlet | 9781914914393 | £6.00
eBook | 9781914914409 | £4.50
1st February 2023

In these rich and witty poems, we encounter a gallery of characters, voices and situations in various stages of emotional undress and bewilderment, fretting at just the wrong distance from reality in railway stations, ferries, restaurants, war zones and watery dystopias. They are filmic pieces that announce the arrival of an unusually gifted poet, in a short collection much bigger than its size – entertaining, disturbing and despite the odds curiously life-affirming.

Here, Miller makes seemingly mundane scenes and interactions extraordinary, with stunning language and unforgettable images. Past Imperfect, Future Tense showcases remarkable skills in exploring deep, human relationships.

– Romalyn Ante

Jon Miller lives near Ullapool in the Scottish Highlands and has had poetry published in a wide range of literary magazines as well as being a contributor of book and exhibition reviews and literary journalism. He was formerly editor of Northwords Now, a magazine featuring writing from the north of Scotland. He was short-listed for the Wigtown Poetry Prize in 2021 and awarded joint First Place in the Neil Gunn Poetry Competition 2022.

JON MILLER

A Greek Chorus at the Close of the Tourist Season

This year's crop is on the promenade
Their meat hangs loose under slogans
They amble camel-hoofed in sandals
Their hair ripples in the pastures
They are dazed by tepid pleasures
They sniff the air like blank dogs
They have brought their naked legs
and parade them as Best In Show
Their heartbeats are barely audible
They have eaten of the fruit of the Brainless Tree
They blunder, weightless as helium buffaloes –
we tie them to railings in strong breezes
We cargo them, pack their husks
in ticking rooms of murderous tidiness
We lay them on mattresses that hold
the warmth of octogenarian sex
We plant them on the golf course
We stuff them in wardrobes, stair cupboards
chimneys, sheds, lay them by for winter
We polish our sky each day
We pat our hills into place
We fluff up our forests
Next year we will take their heads
from the shelf, dust them down
rouse them with trumpets, bacon, eggs.

Lost Child

Not the brazen trumpeters
or the flittering sailboats
or in the minds of mariners
with their white-washed eyes
is there a button of hope.

Neither in the small boys roaming
the fogged avenues
called home for tea
returning with birds' nests
and the ruins of puberty.

You become a twitch
in the fingertips of newscasters
or out here where it happened
the midnight click of the latch
the song in the five-barred gate.

The Nurses

Here they come
with smirks and instruments
a-glitter on silver trays

down shining corridors
they unhook terrible jaws
to chant hymns and arias

their blouses are full of milk
they have sharks' teeth
and plump plum faces

steady are the hands
that make anagrams
of your inner organs

at night they work out
with coalminers
and lesser Norse gods

or moonlight
as headless mannequins
in department store windows

in their plimsolls
you won't hear them coming
till they shriek

like sirens from ambulances
the wail of your mother
on the day of your birth

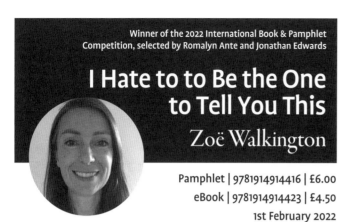

Winner of the 2022 International Book & Pamphlet
Competition, selected by Romalyn Ante and Jonathan Edwards

I Hate to to Be the One to Tell You This

Zoë Walkington

Pamphlet | 9781914914416 | £6.00
eBook | 9781914914423 | £4.50
1st February 2022

It's a shame, isn't it, to have to rat on your neighbours? Upsetting to find out that both your husband and the dog have been telling you lies? And I hate to be the one to tell you this, but there are bad people everywhere, at large, going about their business. Financial insolvents on online-dating sites, contortionist plumbers with a point to prove, and a bloke named Barry, from Halifax, who is singlehandedly ruining the livelihoods of perfectly legitimate psychics. It's not all bad news though, there are Happy Valleys to escape to, ducklings to be held captive by, and that dog, well, you can always put him up for sale. Life, I'm afraid, is based on nothing more than slippery moorings, and this debut pamphlet breaks the bad news with humour and a twist of darkness.

I hate to be the one to tell you *introduces a powerful and distinctive voice. Offering highly original takes on familiar domestic situations, the precise directness of the language creates real comic and emotive impact, in poems crammed with great ideas and unforgettable endings.*

– Jonathan Edwards

Zoë Walkington lives with her whippets in Woburn Sands in Bedfordshire. She is a Professor of Psychology at the Open University, specialising in the psychology of police investigations. She regularly advises the police on interviewing suspects, and acts as an academic advisor to the BBC on factual crime content. Zoë has published poems in *Hinterland*, *Strix*, and *The North* magazines.

Gone Fishing

Maybe I'm thinking too much
but when you tell me you are going fishing
I don't believe you.
You have put a green coat on,
I'll give you that, and wellingtons.
Otherwise, you are dressed as always – sharply.

Your chosen bait the warm cedar tang of Tom Ford.
In your car boot, I don't doubt, your smart shoes.
The only fishing permit obtained,
a reservation for two at Paris House.
Still, I nod and say, *have a nice time*
I hope you catch something.

Washing up, I picture you louche and languid
did you create the right impression?
Or did, during dessert, live fish start to fall
from the ceiling? Perch, roach, salmon and trout
flapping wetly and horribly on your table,
each cold eye looking at nothing.

Ducks

At first they're always under my feet,
peep-peeping and following as I move
from dishwasher to table and back.
They gulp down the grubs and earthworms
I catch, after heavy rain, cutlery fork in hand,
glasses on, standing on one leg like a heron, on the lawn.

Back inside, they circle my feet
peep as loud as tiny whistles
The two bravest peck at my socks with their bills.
I toss worm after worm, grub after grub,
and overnight each duckling's outline expands
as if traced over by a thick pen.

In a week they've doubled in size
and soon they outgrow the washing up bowl,
one always popping over the side.
I move the coffee table and inflate a paddling pool
between my sofas – filling it
with bucket after bucket from the cold tap.
The ducklings bob and splash their content.

Before long the harvest from the back garden
is not enough and I mine the rockery at the front.
The neighbours become inquisitive and I fret
the double glazing will betray me,
the peeps turning into braying quacks.

I become pale. Aldi seems a long way away
and besides, the grubs aren't so bad.
Catching myself in the mirror one day
I brush soil from the corners of my mouth.
My lips harden and crack.

When the paddling pool develops a tear
I put the plug in the sink
move the dishcloth to the granite island,
turn the tap on and wait.
Flooding the floor takes three hours.
Within a day the electrics blow.
We leak surprisingly little, top up just once a day.

Nights are the best. We roost on the granite island
caked with poo. Our breath one rhythm, our feathers puffed.
The two drakes lie awake longer than the rest,
perched on the knife block, blinking into the night.

Winner of the 2022 International Book & Pamphlet Competition, selected by Romalyn Ante and Jonathan Edwards

Dynamo
Luke Samuel Yates

Paperback
| 9781914914430 | £10.99
eBook | 9781914914447 | £6.99
1st March 2023

W hat is *Dynamo*? It is the first full-length collection by an extraordinarily entertaining and exhilarating poet. Over the course of this book, things break down, start again, light up, get stuck. Relationships stagnate, mountains and seas diminish, White nationalists fall over in Blackpool, and a wealthy couple's house disappears one day, leaving them surrounded by their appliances, tanned and eating an egg.

Rich and arresting work. The poet's voice, the language, the imagery: everything is astounding, giving colours to the characters, to the usually ordinary corners of the Midlands, to their hopes and heartaches, and unforgettable narratives.

– Romalyn Ante

Luke Samuel Yates lives in North-West England. He has published two pamphlets (from the Rialto and Smith|Doorstop), was a Poetry Society Foyle Young Poet on four occasions, and was selected for the Aldeburgh Eight. A lecturer in Sociology, he teaches and researches around political movements, technology, and consumption practices.

Persimmon

We took the train
into the mountains
knees under sheets
printed with agricultural motifs

rented a barn
and picked fruit for cash
If people ate more fruit she asks
would they feel less alienated?

I already feel better just being around fruit
just talking about fruit
dearest miniola
my cherimoya

as we share a portion of chips on a wall
the evening settling
like a dog in a dusty room
her hand in mine not really moving

the cars lighting up
sections of trees
lining the B road
on the other side of the valley

people looking for a way
into the next part of their lives.

Can't

When she goes into that silence
he feels like the can opener
that rides around the edge of the can
without opening it in any way.
She could be a can of cool coconut milk.
She could be a can of plum tomatoes.
He is meant to be making a curry.
Settled and progressing in his career.
She is a can of implacable butter beans.
All kinds of possibilities
are slipping away.

They're quite famous, apparently,

although *I* haven't heard of them.
Well that's irrelevant, she says,
which I suppose is true. She's
annoyed about something.

I spend my life working out what.
I drive to the office in my Peugeot in the rain,
in the sun. I eat from a tupperware
looking at my inbox.

Suddenly, she's moving out
and I'm getting into swimming.
Up and down the pool I go, plunging my head
again and again into the water.

POETS I GO BACK TO

For this issue our four 2022/3 Book & Pamphlet Competition winners, **Karen Downs-Barton**, **Jon Miller**, **Zoë Walkington**, and **Luke Samuel Yates** choose the poets who have made a difference to their own writing

KAREN DOWNS-BARTON

The poets I return to share certain traits. Each harnesses language, form, and imagery, constructing worlds to disappear into or recognise yourself through. Sarah Wimbush is a good example of the latter. Her poem, 'Bloodlines', feels like a mirror held up, I see 'the need to set the curtains ajar at night', the lineage traced 'in a handful of photographs and crumpled vowels' and think, 'Ah yes, there I am.' 'Bloodlines' form is a joy. It appears concrete but try to define the shape … It refuses to be defined. The visceral imagery of 'Earring' its pinched lobe pierced, a thread pulled 'now and then to clear the hole so the flesh doesn't grow' always makes me squirm.

My touchstone for ekphrastic poetry is Pascale Petit's *What the Water Gave Me*. Frida Kahlo's paintings inform Petit's collection of elegant and startling poetry. After reading 'My Birth' the line '(l)ook at how I wear my mother's body like a regional dress' haunted me. That's great writing as is the collections narrative arc. The last poem opens 'This is how it is at the end' and closes 'don't make me come back.' This bold strategy offer readers permission to close the book but raises the suggestion of a mutual haunting; the reader by Kahlo's/Petit's imagery and Kahlo summoned back by our gaze.

Last but by no means least is Edwin Morgan's, *Collected Poems*, 'ain Frankenstein for metamorphosis' of language and form, texture and tone. I return to Morgan's sequences time-and-again. I first encountered him through 'The Glasgow Sonnets', their 'places with no windows left to smash' and life's 'bric-a-brac'.

Another not-to-be-missed sequence is 'An Alphabet of Goddesses'; such layers and imagery in 'long tight boots' and girdles like 'a brace of promises'. But Morgan's poems are also meditations on language and the potential of a single word. In 'The Moment of Death' one word 'unite' morphs along the page, ultimately dissolving as 'untie.' Wonderful!

P. Petit *What The Water Gave Me*, Seren
E. Morgan, *Collected Poems*, Carcanet.
S. Wimbush, *Shelling Peas with My Grandmother in the Gorgiolands*, Bloodaxe.

JON MILLER

At times the poets I go back to are those that help me write more poems. When my brain needs a jump start, some defibrillation. To use the orbit of another planet to hurl me further out. When I need to hear the voice of someone I trust leading me through a hard place when I don't know what it is I'm writing or how the hell I'm going to get out the other side.

So - James Tate, Mary Ruefle, Charles Simic rush to the front unbidden. All three startle and confound with their imagery, their juxtapositions, their sudden shifts of angle of approach as if from the back of the sun, emerging from some unforeseen *Interstellar* parallelism in their the particularisation of detail, bizarre time shifts. They each give me the presumption to throw out a line and follow it as far as I can knowing that if James or Mary or Charles has gone there then so can

Mary's poems are pieces of life slipping through your fingers, fingers you maybe never had in the first place.

I, that they are out there to catch me and pass me on.

Quoting lines is a dangerous business with them but here's a few, randomly:

'Late that night it rained so hard the world/seemed flattened for good' (Mary)
'His clock has stopped watching./His watch, an immense presence/an octopus with jewels'. (James)
'Happiness, you are the bright red lining/Of the dark winter coat/Grief wears inside out.' (Charles)

James' *The Rally* is the funniest, most apposite and off-kilter poem for these polarised times. Mary's poems are pieces of life slipping through your fingers, fingers you maybe never had in the first place. Charles' poems bustle with ants and malevolent cutlery.

I suppose this is a kind of mini-Avenger origin story. You'll notice I've used their first names. That's how close we are. Which is pretty creepy.

ZOË WALKINGTON

The first poetry pamphlet I ever held in my hands, was Matthew Clegg's *Nobody sonnets*. The pamphlet, published by Longbarrow Press in 2008, is physically quite small and contains just twelve poems alongside illustrations by Andrew Hirst. I had just started writing poetry myself, guided by Mark Doyle who was running workshops in Penistone. Mark gave me the pamphlet as a gift, said he was sure I would like it. I didn't know what a poetry pamphlet was at the time. Even before I opened it, it seemed to be something magical and precious.

Around eleven years later it is still my favourite pamphlet. Clegg's deft sketches of individuals, often down on their luck, hit that illusive sweet spot of being both comic, yet crafted with empathy.

'As if being divorced, out of work and living
In his parents' box room wasn't plenty
To be going on with. He'd been taking

Some solace over a lager one Sunday'
(from Pups # 1: Paul)

I was thrilled by the commonplace language. I didn't, at the time, realise poetry could be like that, with lines running over, like a conversation down at the pub. Returning to Clegg's work today, having read a little more poetry, there are new things to appreciate: The way his observations of everyday behaviour fit so neatly and quietly into his chosen form.

To me, the last four lines from *Open to the sky* (the final poem in *Nobody sonnets*) illustrates not only Clegg's skill as a writer, but also my feelings about the gifts, as poets, we give one another. The beauty that is to be found in the ordinary, and the joy there is in noticing it.

We live on what we find. Like crows. Like gulls.
The sun sinks and the landfill loses colour.
Lacking anything else, two teenage girls
Take photo after photo of each other.

LUKE SAMUEL YATES

In Issue 68 this feature invited poets, *and* artists, to reflect on artists, not only poets, they go back to. 'Influence', declared the guest editors Andrew McMillan and Stephanie Sy-Quia, 'is often spoken of too narrowly'. Thinking about artists, cartoonists, musicians, they say, 'invites more generous ways of thinking about influence and tradition'. Then in the section itself there's some very nice writing about choreography and manga comics. Yes. Another reason why I agree with this, though, is because outside-poetry influences are so burstingly obvious and exciting in some of the poets I've found myself re-reading in the last year or two, in the books that spend more time off the bookshelf than on it: David Berman, better known as lyricist and songwriter of the Silver Jews; Matt Welton, whose music tastes also seem excellent and whose delicious sequences remind me very much

I was thrilled by the commonplace language. I didn't, at the time, realise poetry could be like that ...

95

of the playful, halting, circular dialogue of Hal Hartley films and the short stories of Donald Barthelme and perhaps Quim Monzó; and Heather Phillipson, whose art I find as enjoyable as her writing (I just opened on and re-read 'The Horse Jacuzzi' from with much delight because I have *Instant-flex 718* on my desk right here, her art and violin- and piano-playing must also be somewhere in there). The patterns of reference and influence in re-reading also happen outside of reading: there's a bird in nearly every Robert Hass poem, and I came across him (via a video algorithm, a newer form of influence and cultural indexing with a lot of power) before I learned the names and the habits of the birds who live in the closest woodland to where I live. Now, thinking about either birds or Robert Hass is somehow enhanced by, and indexes the pleasures and particularities of, the other. And it's the echoes of Chekhov which I think eased me into the films of Asghar Farhadi and early Joanna Hogg, and the poems of Lee Harwood. John Cage, meanwhile, refused to acknowledge any relationship at all between his musical compositions and his expertise in mushrooms, a position I respect.

Now, thinking about either birds or Robert Hass is somehow enhanced by, and indexes the pleasures and particularities of, the other.

THE LONDON MAGAZINE

Est. 1732

Hello! This is *The London Magazine*, the UK's oldest literary periodical. We publish poetry, short fiction, essays, and reviews. Past contributors include T. S. Eliot, Hilary Mantel, Sylvia Plath, Helen Dunmore, Christopher Reid, Isabel Galleymore, and Raymond Antrobus, to name a few. Fancy subscribing? **Here's an exclusive offer** for *The North* readers. . .

SUBSCRIPTION BUNDLE

Receive 10% off select TLM subscriptions

+

1 free limited-edition tote bag

+

A complimentary issue from our archive

USE DISCOUNT CODE: THENORTH

(Offer available for a limited time only)

Search: thelondonmagazine.org/subscription

 thelondonmagazine @*TheLondonMag*

 thelondonmagazine1732 *thelondonmagazine.org*

Gina Wilson (1943–2022)

We asked four of Gina's writer friends to choose a poem to respond to. Three of these are poets who are also her publishers, Helena Nelson of Happen*Stance* and Hamish Whyte and Diana Hendry of Mariscat. They are joined here by James Caruth who, like us, was so glad to know Gina from workshops and residentials – where, as well as being an extraordinarily gifted and generous writer and reader, she was also excellent and often slightly mischievous company. One memory we have is of a first evening at a writing weekend in the Lake District, when Gina, finding the bar not yet open, promptly shimmied over the counter to return to Ann Sansom with a bottle of white and two glasses.

In addition to her own poem choice, Helena Nelson has found an unpublished piece, which seems fitting to print at the head of this celebration of the remarkable Gina Wilson.

Night Cafe

She didn't turn me away.
The night was too wet and black.
There was nowhere to go.

'I was going to lock up,' she said.
'The place has been empty for hours.'

She brought coffee, sat beside me,
pulled up a chair for our feet.

'Do you want to tell me anything,
a young girl like you?'

I shook my head. 'Nothing to say.'
'Always something,' she said.

Later she started to nod.
'Let's get some sleep,' she said.
'We need it.'

For her sake I closed my eyes.
When I opened them, she was staring.
'How can I help you?' she said.

HELENA NELSON

I have an untestable theory that sometimes poets trap a little bit of themselves in a poem, a fragment of the spirit. When you read such a piece, it lights up — like the filament of an old-fashioned lightbulb —and for a few seconds the author is right there. An example, for me, is Keats's 'This Living Hand', the one that eerily ends, 'I hold it towards you'.

'Before I go', by Gina Wilson, is one of those poems too. Given the poet's death last year, the title may seem poignant, though I doubt Gina was thinking about mortality when she wrote it, and it may have been written a decade ago. She was just preparing to leave a house she loved, a place of rich textures and associations. Her plan was to 'walk naked' through the building, soaking it in.

If you google her image online, you'll see Gina tended to wear scarves looped around her neck, on top of a blouse or pullover. She wasn't a bare-skin sort of person, at least not so far as I could see, so 'I will walk naked' is an arresting opening line, a daring statement for her.

But for me, it's not until line five that the poem really takes off. It starts to bite when she says: 'How can I ever leave? Others can't.' That's where the magic begins.

She goes on to talk about the house's curious inhabitants and, in so doing, reveals much about the place.

Gina published *Scissors, Paper, Stone* (Happen*Stance* 2010) and *It Was and It Wasn't* (Mariscat 2017), which was shortlisted for the Michael Marks Poetry Pamphlet Award. Other publications include young adult novels (Faber), children's poetry (Cape) and picture books (Walker).

It has a hall with tiles, a cobwebby wine cellar, an attic, a guest room fit for a prime minister. As for the ghosts, she clearly welcomes them. In fact, when she says 'I'll drift, in my private openness' she sounds like a ghost herself. 'Private openness' — what a beautiful phrase! She's about to expose her 'wide-awake skin', which is 'nerved to remember'. Her words are familiar and strange, accessible and mysterious.

Poets often draw on the senses, especially sight, sound, smell and taste. Focussing only on touch is unusual. Think tangible, and you think finger-tips. But this poem-experience is processed though the whole skin (the largest organ of the human body). It's something more complex than ordinary touch, perhaps a way of imprinting the house so she can keep it inside her, and keep herself inside it. I think she's stepped out of time. That's partly why she's writing in the future tense, about what she is going to do but hasn't yet done. The experience is putative. And yet in the closing line, she jumps suddenly into the present: 'the touch *is* here' [italics mine].

In fact, the whole concluding stanza is more than a little strange. 'When time and space reclothe me' is an odd way of saying 'when I put my clothes back on'. But that's not what she's saying. It's not just dress. It's the whole mortal coil: messy human existence inside time and space. Naked in the house, in her poem, she's temporarily elsewhere — somewhere spiritual, I think. How can she ever leave? She hasn't. Not quite. The airy sound-echo in the last line between 'here' and 'air' is her ghost, her living breath, her lingering sigh.

Before I go

I'll walk naked
through this tall-windowed house,
feel its rooms draw me into embraces
velvet, leather, silk.

How can I ever leave? Others can't.
Not the lone mouse pattering the hall-tiles,
nor the thread-legged spiders

sheeting the wine cellar,
nor the maid who flits nightly

from attic to basement.
Even Gladstone, who stayed just once,
still dumps his bag on the guest-room floor
and paces.

I'll drift, in my private openness,
down passages, through doorways
with wide-awake skin nerved
to remember.

When time and space reclothe me
the touch is here:
these boards and walls, this air.

HAMISH WHYTE

It Was and It Wasn't was to me an especially pleasing Mariscat pamphlet – green typographical cover, grey endpapers and typefaces (Bulmer and Perpetua) carefully chosen by our designer Gerry Cambridge. A nice, compact collection of 22 poems: spare, unsentimental (but often moving), unsettling and humorous. As the blurb says, you are lured into thinking you're on safe, possibly domestic territory, but then you're caught unawares, taken off at an unexpected tangent. One of my favourites is the short poem 'Treasure', from which the title of the collection comes: ordinary stuff, squirrels burying nuts, leading to the mother and Christmas dates and nuts she couldn't leave unopened; then to the brother digging up their dead rabbit by torchlight 'to see if it was safe.' It was and it wasn't – the punchline says it all.

I love Gina's matter-of-fact tone. The clear-eyed psychotherapist who's seen and heard it all – and tells you without (obvious) judgement.

The pamphlet was shortlisted for the Michael Marks Poetry Award, the ceremony, in December 2018, at the British Library. Diana and I met Gina and her husband

Edward for a drink before the event at Carluccio's in St Pancras Station and spent a delightful hour in their company. During the evening she was grateful to Diana going round our table and sitting in a gap to engage a woman from the *TLS* 'thereby pretty well forcing Declan Ryan to talk to me!'

She wrote to us to say she didn't mind not winning and that she and Edward had a wonderful day. 'Got home at 1a.m.'

Treasure

Squirrels spend a lot of time
digging up and reburying their store,
checking it's still there, taking a bite.
My mother used to be the same
with dates and nuts at Christmas.
Never an unopened box of anything
by the Day itself. Funny how people
can't quite bury a treasure. My brother
dug up our dead rabbit by torchlight
to see if it was safe. It was and it wasn't.

DIANA HENDRY

One of the things which I felt Gina and I had in common and which added to my liking of her, is that we both wrote for children. Gina published an impressive range of books for children of all ages, her books being shortlisted for the Carnegie medal, the Kurt Maschler Award and the Smarties Prize.

I've chosen 'Child's Play' because it tells a children's story but tells it as simply as if it were a picture book text before hitting you with its clean, fierce psychological insight. It's a poem about the cruelty of children, a subject many have written about, but here, as the narrator's awful but casual confession it possesses a shocking force. Simultaneously the reader realises the pretend innocence and knowingness of the narrator's *My mummy's coming to collect me soon* and the stabbing hurt inflicted on the bereaved five-year when asked *Is yours?*

A Gina Wilson poem starts off nonchalantly – almost with an air of wide-eyed innocence – and then takes you either on a flight of imagination or to or a unexpected insight. I thought the title of her Mariscat collection, 'It Was and It Wasn't' was somehow terribly appropriate for a psychotherapist.

Gina came to visit us at home for Mariscat's almost traditional editorial session. Next time we met it was because she'd been short-listed for the Michael Marks Award. We had a most enjoyable supper with her and her husband at the British Library. Gina seemed entirely unbothered about not winning and was simply pleased to be there.

I wish I'd spent more time with her.

Child's Play

You're lucky said Gran,
not like the little soul next door.
She was five, staying with her gran too;
her mum had just died.

They wonder if you'll go and play.

Play with a five year old!
I was seven.
Be kind said Gran.

I remember being there —
parched grass, windfalls, heat,
I remember her — limp frock, empty hands,
how I drew her to the garden's end.

It's nice staying with grans, isn't it? I said.
*My mummy's coming to collect me soon.
Is yours?*

A Gina Wilson poem starts off nonchalantly – almost with an air of wide-eyed innocence – and then takes you either on a flight of imagination or to or a unexpected insight.

JAMES CARUTH

I first met Gina Wilson at a Poetry Business event and was lucky enough to be with her on several Poetry Writing Weeks run by PB at Rydal Hall in Ambleside. Living in Oxford and having to submit to the vagaries of the British rail services, the journey to the Lake District could be long and complicated for her. It was then I suggested she should come to Sheffield by train and I would give her a lift (and some company) for the rest of the trip.

I remember those journeys filled with conversation, always interesting and insightful as the miles passed. Gina was an excellent poet and helpful critic, her poems refusing any labelling, touching on issues at times difficult or unsettling for the reader but always tender and honest.

One particular instance I recall was at the end of such a Writing Week in 2016, that last read around of poems that we had finished during the week. I remember the room at Rydal, the group around a square of tables, sunlight through the windows, the red squirrels inquisitive on their feeding station.

Gina's turn to read, that small piping voice, not words but birdsong she had listened to that morning in the Hall's sculptured gardens. A found poem of sorts, given to her by the robins, tits, goldfinches and the one solitary blackbird. She had an ear for the music of words. I still try and follow her advice, still try and listen *do*.

Gina's turn to read, that small piping voice, not words but birdsong she had listened to that morning in the Hall's sculptured gardens.

Tutti
7.15 am. Birds above Rydal Water 29/5/16

oi oi oi oi

I keep trrrilling this. It's imporrrtant. Is anyone hearrring? I keep trrrilling this

       ahoy there   I'm off   come too
   yeeeah .....yeeeah .....
me doh   me doh   me doh

I keep trrrilling this. It's important. Is anyone hearrring? I keep trrrilling this
oi oi oi oi
       cooee? cooee? cooee?
trrrrrrrrrrrrrrrrrr

     yaaaak   yaaaak

I keep ...

me doh   me doh   me doh

     ouk! ouk!
tooooot
  tiramisu
      listen *do*   listen *do*

About the Authors

Helena Nelson's publications include the reading and writing guide *Unlocked* and collections such as *Starlight on Water* and *Pearls*.

Diana Hendry has published many books for children and her poetry books include two recent collections from Worple Press, *The Watching Stair* and *The Guest Room*.

Hamish Whyte has recently published the memoir *Morgan and Me* and collections of poems including *Testimonies* and *Paper Cut* (Shoestring).

James Caruth's most recent book, *Speechless at Inch* (Smith|Doorstop), was shortlisted for the Derek Walcott Prize.

POETRY
Book
Society

JOIN NOW

* START YOUR YEAR OF POETRY DISCOVERY
* ENJOY THE BEST NEW POETRY BOOKS
* CURATED & DELIVERED TO YOUR DOOR
* INSPIRING QUARTERLY POETRY MAGAZINES
* PLUS A FREE BOOK FOR NEW MEMBERS

WWW.POETRYBOOKS.CO.UK

Longbarrow Press

Four years after *The Grail Roads* appeared to wide acclaim, **Rob Hindle**'s fourth collection resounds with calls and 'siren notes' which are strange and familiar, settled and contingent. *Sapo* is available now in hardback from Longbarrow Press.

Longbarrow Press is an independent poetry publisher whose work explores the intersections of landscape, history and memory. Recent books include *This is a Picture of Wind* by J.R. Carpenter and *The European Eel* by Steve Ely. New titles by Angelina D'Roza and Helen Tookey will appear in autumn 2023.

www.longbarrowpress.com

Sapo

Orpheus returned to the world songless and broken.
People watched and said nothing, knowing
his wife was lost. One day they'd tell stories:
how he chased her beyond death, brought her
out of the earth and clutched her to him

till at dawn a neighbour found them in the garden
inarticulate. Autumn has come down from the north
with its poems and shadows, its old memories.
Each year we shrink from the journey,
gather like moths round lamps, dance at the dark.

Everything quietens and slows. Some live on;
some, dying, persist as seeds, bones, spores.
We are rich with life and can't outrun it.
Better to settle as the toad settles,
believing in his end and his endless nativity.

FEATURED TITLE

Out of Sri Lanka
Tamil, Sinhala and English poetry from Sri Lanka and its diasporas
Edited by Shash Trevett, Sensi Seneviratne and Vidyan Ravinthiran
Bloodaxe Books 424pp
£14.99

This first ever anthology of Sri Lankan and diasporic poetry – many exiles refuse to identify as "Sri Lankan" – features over a hundred poets writing in English, or translated from Tamil and Sinhala. It brings to light a long-neglected national literature, and reshapes our understanding of migrational poetics and the poetics of atrocity. Poets long out of print appear beside exciting new talents; works written in the country converse with poetry from the UK, the US, Canada and Australia.

There are poems here about love, art, nature – and others exploring critical events: the Marxist JVP insurrections of the 1970s and 80s, the 2004 tsunami and its aftermath, recent bombings linked with the demonisation of Muslim communities. The civil war between the government and the separatist Tamil Tigers is a haunting and continual presence. A poetry of witness challenges those who would erase, rather than enquire into, the country's troubled past. This anthology affirms the imperative to remember, whether this relates to folk practices suppressed by colonisers, or more recent events erased from the record by Sinhalese nationalists.

AAZHIYAAL

Unheeded Sights

After the rains
the tiled roofs shone
sparklingly clean.
The sky was not yet minded
to become a deeper blue.
The tar roads reminded me
intermittently of rainbows.
From the entire surface of the earth
a fine smoke arose
like the smoke of frankincense, or akil wood,
the earth's scent stroking the nostrils,
fragrant as a melody.

As the army truck coming towards me
drives away,
a little girl transfers her candy-floss
from one hand to the other
raises her right hand up high
and waves her tiny fingers.

And like the sweet surprise
of an answering air-letter
all the soldiers standing in the truck
wave their hands, exactly like her.
The blood that froze in my veins
for an instant, in amazement,
flows again rapidly, asking aloud,
'War? In this land?
Who told you?'

[tr. from Tamil by Lakshmi Holmström]

The Big Wave

The boat is made of coconut palms:
a wooden whale hollowed out
with two ribs stuck in a second hull.
A fisherman's rough catamaran.

Kapu perched on the outrigger
would sail into the night, but not too far.
His lamp, he knows from his father's short life,
must always be seen from the shore,

'Malu, malu, malu,
dhang genapu malu,
Suranganita malu genavaa ...'
Fish, fish, fish, he sings,
just brought in,
for Surangani I have brought fresh fish.
A simple song that rises from the dark
lisping coastline,
a hungry heart,
an offering of netted moonlight.

This morning when he rides back
on the slow deep swell,
he comes with no slivers from the moon.
Not a single one.
He pulls the boat up the beach,
his brother and his son,
their shoulders to the two ribs,
nudge it out of the water's reach.
'Koheda malu?' his Surangani asks,
tightening the green cloth
around her waist.
Where is the fish?

Kapu brings out his empty net.
'Puduma vade, malu na.'
Strange business, no fish.
It is a mystery to him.

His son curls his toes in the white sand.
What could have happened to the moon?
Where would the fish go?
The blue line of the sea
marks the end of the world.

WIMAL DISSANAYAKE

Homecoming

My grandmother, silver-haired and frail,
sitting on a mat, with the betel tray next to her,
used to spin endless tales
in those monsoon evenings, when
dark ropes of dusk coiled in the air.
My brother and I were turned into
silent statues of clay, kneaded in her narratives.
She told us stories of kings and demons,
beasts and flowers; one evening, I remember well,
a bird escaped from her story, rose to the sky,
flapped its wings, flew higher and higher, and
disappeared like a dot in the darkening sky.
Forty years later, the bird has come back,
wiser, if a little weaker, to roost in my mind.
It's a large bird with a long beak
and brown feathers. I'll show it to my kids
when they come back from school.

[tr. from Sinhala by the poet]

ANNE RANASINGHE

July 1983

I used to wonder
about the Nazi killers,
and those who stood and watched the killing:

does the memory
of so many pleading eyes
stab like lightning through their days and years

and do the voices
of orphaned children
weeping forlornly before dying

haunt their nights?
are their nights sleepless –
has the agony and anguish and

the blood and terror and pain
carved a trail in their brain
saying: I am guilty. Never again …

Forty years later
once more there is burning
the night sky bloodied, violent and abused

and I – though related
only by marriage –
feel myself both victim and accused,

(black-gutted timber
splinters, shards and ashes
blowing in the wind: nothing remains)—

flinch at the thinnest curl of smoke
shrink from the merest thought of fire
while some warm their hands at the flames.

from *Excellence*

The food cooked by Thevayaanai
was always delicious. Her touch
transformed plain aubergine
into shark curry. Words couldn't capture
the elegance of that good woman's
lentils when swelled with ghee.
Her fortunate husband's full belly
added inches to his waist.

On Fridays she nagged him
to go to the fish market.
He exhaled his reply.
He woke at eight each morning.
Was there anything he couldn't accomplish
in a day? Would they ever go without?
She cooked him delicious crab.
With thankfulness he gobbled it up.

[...]

Muththaiyan sent his mother's medicines
in a letter to his father.
He gave parties for his close friends
adding sparkle to their lives.
To prevent time from turning him
into a withered mango tree
he wandered the streets, searching
for newer, bigger houses to rent.

When he reclaimed the jewellery already pawned
he remembered the wise words of his father:
'Boy, you have only studied sufficiently
once tomorrow's lesson is over' —
His heart was overcome.

'Look to Shiva' his father had advised.
'Look after your health' – this had become
his mother's mantra.

[...]

Finishing work he would turn for home.
Waiting in a queue, his thoughts
circled around Thevayaanai.
If he had sufficient change in his pocket
he bought some laddus. Street after street
opened before him, but shutting his nose
to the distracting aromas he would hurry home.
Reaching the sari shop he would promise himself:
'After I get paid'.

[...]

[tr from Tamil by Shash Trevett]

The Poet

i

am the eye of the camera
can only reflect, never reject,
never deflect

i

am the eye
of the camera
silent recorder of life
and death
eye that can only reflect
never conjure up images
probe the reality
never reject

i am the eye
of the camera
i reflect nothing
but truth

the external reality
cannot deflect
the mind of the viewer
from picture to passion

i let them all fashion
their truths through my magic
I cannot reject
the external reality
that passes for truth

and what is rejected
by natural selection
has nothing to do with me
when i am impotent
robbed of my power
my eyes in the dark at the moment of crisis
see nothing but well favoured men of the hour

i

am the storm's eye
ceaselessly turning
around me the burning the death the destruction
the clichés that govern the world of the words
of the prophets and preachers, and maybe the saviours
are lost to my peering
blind eye in the dark

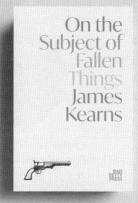

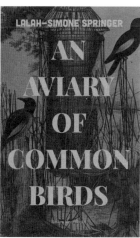

'Too early at the custard factory'

New & Selected Poems
Cliff Yates
Paperback | 978-1-914914-59-1 | £10.99
eBook | 978-1-914914-60-7 | £6.99
July 2023

Cliff Yates's New & Selected Poems brings together over thirty years of inimitable work, from his Fenton Aldeburgh Prize debut, Henry's Clock, to his most recent pamphlet, Another Last Word and beyond. His poems are moving, surprising and funny, sometimes in the space of a few lines, and, gathered together wonderfully here, add up to an oblique but compelling document of lives and times.

Cliff Yates is one of my favourite poets, writing in an idiom I'd like to call "Skelmersdale Mystic/Domestic." If he was in a band that band would produce hit singles that would linger in your head for years and if he was a greengrocer his vegetables would always be startling shapes. There's childhood here, and love, and a way of seeing the world with the wrappers off that is, ultimately, Yatesian.

    – Ian McMillan

These lucid and nimble poems effortlessly thread in and out of the quotidian, exuding a wry, wise vitality that is entirely their own.

    – Scott Thurston

Cliff Yates was born in Birmingham and grew up in Birmingham and Kidderminster. He left school at 16 for the printing factory and did various jobs before returning to full time education. He taught English at Maharishi School, where his students were renowned for winning poetry competitions. Awards for his poetry include the Fenton Aldeburgh First Collection Prize, the Poetry Business Book & Pamphlet Competition, and an Arts Council England Writers Award. He wrote *Jumpstart Poetry in the Secondary School* during his time as Poetry Society poet-in-residence. A hugely experienced writing tutor, he is a former Royal Literary Fund Fellow at Aston University.

Fifteen

Philip Aston was born middle-aged:
Brylcreem and cycle clips, a faint moustache,
like somebody's dad or one of the teachers.
Here he is in the bike shed, chaining up his RSW,
fifteen years old in his prefect's blazer.

Prefects. Roger gave us twenty-five lines
for mucking about, then we talked him out of it.
I saw him recently, called in at the farm.
He told me how they found their dad
in the cowshed. That's how he wants to go.

The barn I creosoted when I was fifteen
is still standing and hasn't been creosoted since.
Their Cedric showed me how to drive.
We followed a track round the edge of a field.
He had to turn off the radio. A good record
made me go faster, I didn't realise. It still does.

They'll never make me a prefect –
the special blazer, the badge – not in this lifetime,
hanging about the bike sheds, waiting for something
to happen, or singing along in the outside lane, eighty-five, ninety.

Eagle Special Investigator

In Longfields charity shop on Bath Road
I find a copy of *Eagle Special Investigator*
I used to have when I was a kid. Macdonald
Hastings. In the black & white photos
he's wearing glasses like the ones
back in fashion that looked old-fashioned then.
He looks like somebody's dad (but everybody did),
Hank Marvin before Hank Marvin. The cover's
unfamiliar: mostly yellow (some red), Eagle logo,
Macdonald H. bottom right, thumbnail head
and shoulders in a cowboy hat.

I've thought about this book on and off
over the years and maybe I was hungry
when I read it but the only part
I remembered apart from the title
was the size of the lumberjack's breakfast.

'Mines for Gold' has him prospecting for gold
in Canada and being free with the comma:
I got the fever, over a plate of pork hock,
with Bill Johnson and Wally Brinks,
and after Bill Johnson's tale of the old days
when twenty-seven mules came in from Eldorado
piled up with gold like grain and so much gold
inside the banks they stacked it outside in bags:
I couldn't imagine why I'd wasted my time
as a Special Investigator. 'How do I start?' I said.

Spitfires were built in Castle Bromwich

1. Thinktank Birmingham 2019 / Aircraft factory 1940

Iconic the shape
above us, the spread
of the wings

Let's hear it for the women
of the engine production line
the lathe, the drill, the milling machine

Sit in the cut-away cockpit
pull back the lever, press
the red button
for the muffled drone

For the mechanics, riggers and fitters
assembling Spitfires in the assembly shed

Falafel sandwiches, mugs of tea
and a Penguin, all we need
as out on the street
snow turns to ice

For the sunken rivets and the elliptical wing
For the first test run –
the precision roll and the vertical climb

No grip, and we're single file
on the pavement, holding onto the rail
shouting to be heard
shouting into the cold

Panning shot of Spitfire flying at speed

2. Fisher & Ludlow, Castle Bromwich (former aircraft factory) 1950

Mum in the offices,
Dad on a job there,
carpenter and joiner.

She notices how his boots are shiny
('a man who cleans his shoes …')
how he's always neat and clean –

collar and tie, brown denim overalls,
pencil behind his ear.
And respectful, they're not all like that.

'Would you like to come to the dance?'
'No,' she said, 'I can't dance.'
'I can teach you.'

Waiting for Caroline

Outside Readings on Blackwell Street,
bikes in one window, jokes in this one:
nail through your finger, Frankenstein,
invisible ink. She looked great
behind the gym at dinner time.
Her friends were in the long jump pit
out of sight of the dinner ladies,
holding down Andy and giving him love
bites. Outside Fletcher's, Mr Fletcher
humps potatoes, sings in Italian. She's late.

I've been set up, like Cary Grant
in *North by North West*
                    I'll hear it
before I see it, the crop duster
out of the sun above the multi-storey
dipping dangerously over the Seven Stars.
I'll make it to the Red Cross on Silver Street,
under the ambulance, hands over my ears ...
On the way home, the fat man in the black suit
will climb on the Stourport bus with his cello.

I imagine her coming round the corner
by the Riverboat, she's run from the bus stop
but she's not sweating, she's smiling
like the girl in the Flake advert.

I'll tell John I didn't turn up
and if Frog says anything I'll hit him.

Lifting

Too early at the Custard Factory
for the lunch and too late for breakfast,
the towpath's closed at Broad Street, the Ikon
galleries are shut, and it doesn't look good
for our Digbeth jerry can hardware shop
but dodge between buildings
more or less opposite the bus station
for the five workmen and mini digger
laying paving in a dream, the foreman
on his knees, smoothing sand with bare hands
in front of the thirty-foot GARAGE DOORS
brick wall and, half-way up, the blue sign
              No lifting
              over this
              building
the dark green canister, the red board –
a composition, a film set, abstract painting.
All over Brum they're laying new paving.

John Foggin (1943-2023)

We were very sorry to hear of the death of John Foggin, an outstanding poet and remarkable man, whom we were proud to publish, and whose friendship we cherished. He will be greatly missed by many people, not least his former students and the poets he worked with and encouraged.

The (truly) Great Fogginzo's Cobweb can be found at johnfogginpoetry.com. Calder Valley Press have produced a festschrift, *Dear Foggs*. They also published John's last book, which is reviewed here by David Constantine. The piece was written before John's death, and we are glad to say that John did get to read it.

In the meantime

because that's how it is, the sparrow
flying into the meadhall, bewildered
by smoke-reek, gusts of beer-breath,
out of the wild dark and into the half-
light of embers, sweat, the steam
of fermenting rushes, and maybe
a harp and an epic that means nothing
in a language it doesn't know, this sparrow,
frantic to be out there, and maybe
it perches on a tarry roof beam, catches
a wingtip, comes up against thatch
like a moth on a curtain, and it beats
its wings, it beats its wings, it tastes
a wind with the scent of rain, the thin
smell of snow, of stars, and somehow
it's out into the turbulence of everywhere,
and who knows what happens next.

DAVID CONSTANTINE

John Foggin, *Pressed for Time*, 104pp, £14.20, Calder Valley Poetry, 2022

I'll start with a well-known truth which in these disintegrating and atomizing times wants telling again and again. It is this: the peculiar good poetry does consists in giving us entry into lives which are not ours, are perhaps remote in time and kind from ours, but which will, if let, quicken and expand our own. The poet – here John Foggin – writing feelingly and exactly about things local and home to him (clarifying them and their value to him as he writes), enriches us doing so, widens our sympathies. That's the heart of it, that other human lives can be touched on, attached to, brought into a multiplicity of relations, beyond those of the I they belonged to in the beginning.

As it happens (my good luck) I share many of John Foggin's beloved localities and likes and dislikes. But coming across them in his work my reaction is certainly not, 'Ah, I know all about that'. Yes, there's the lovely shock of recognition, but it is mixed with Lear's realization in the storm on the heath, 'O, I have ta'en/ Too little care of this!'. He sees he knows nothing of how the wretched live. But his suddenly knowing that he has paid too little attention to the lot of other human beings, his *opening*, might, of course, be applied to the countless occurrences and phenomena we do not adequately attend to. I felt it again and again in reading this collection, and was on every occasion grateful.

Pressed for Time is not so much haunted by mortality as urged by the fact of it to gather in valuable past experiences, many out of the depths of childhood, into a living present, where, difficult though some are, each in its own fashion may be a help. Another way of

... the peculiar good poetry does consists in giving us entry into lives which are not ours, are perhaps remote in time and kind from ours, but which will, if let, quicken and expand our own.

putting it is that a multitude of things, creatures (not just human), localities and past and present events *want saying*. I mean 'want' in two senses: desire and need. In my list only humans can actually desire or need this saying. Whether they know it, admit it, or not, human beings, some oftener than others, want things said. We feel that life will be wanting unless at least some of its infinite abundance is said. John Foggin's book is jampacked with urgent sayings. For example, there's a tally of employments, named ways of being in the world in the public view which make you liable to be remembered and assessed: school-teacher, miner, hangman, doctor, comedian … All livingly summoned up, very present. Best of these, in my view, is 'Night Soil Man'. The man and his horse are being brought to life as they are being said – by him in the poem, and by the poet pressed to say him:

> When all this is over, said the night soil man,
> I'll make a fire, sift ashes, boil up lye and scour
> the cart, holystone it white as bone. Then burn
> my working clothes, my boots, my spade and rake.
>
> I'll currycomb the old horse, I'll braid his mane
> and oil his hoofs. The cart I'll paint with roses,
> like a varda or a narrowboat, and we'll ride out
> past Beeston, past the forcing sheds,
>
> find a quiet place where he can graze, and I'll imagine
> I can smell the grass. Scent is a language
> I shall relearn, said the night soil man:
> lavender, sage and cedar; woodsmoke, lemons.
>
> I shall shed this skin, I shall whiten, soften,
> sleep light in clean linen, with an ear for the grind
> of iron-shod wheels on cobbles in the lane,
> the scrape of pails, the snuffling of the horse.
>
> Some afternoons, I'll take the cart and ride
> up ginnels, the backs of decent terraces.
> I'll look down into yards where men grow leeks,
> pink-stemmed rhubarb, scarlet-flowered beans.

> And I shall learn the scents of the world again.
> The elusive ones: clean sweat, petrichor,
> air before snow, like tin. The essence of a baby,
> the blue pulse in her skull I'll be let to kiss.

A central subject of this volume is illness, hospitals, treatments. The writer, in pain of his own, attends acutely and precisely to the sufferings of others. As here in 'High Dependency', an aptly *drifting* poem:

> I'm split like a fig parched as old newsprint
> listening to Mrs Mumtaz's murmuring daughters
> longing for sweet sips of water in a shimmer
> of saffron plum and emerald chinks and gleams
> of gold of bracelets finely threaded scarves
> the exact and beautiful pleats of the turban
> of Mr Mumtaz who sits by the ghost of his wife
> cobwebbed with morphine and the whispers
> of slender daughters exotic and wary as birds
> embroidering me dreams where no staples pluck
> where there are no drains or snaky tubes
> no oscillating screens no stupidity of pain
> that's somewhere in this room and might be mine.

The book has six parts, the last of them, called *Epilogue*, being just one poem, 'In the Meantime', which radically reworks Bede's likening a human life to the brief passage of a sparrow through a warm and hospitable hall. Foggin's bird feels trapped in that enclosed haven, is 'frantic to be out there', out again in 'the turbulence of everywhere'. So this final poem is not an epilogue at all really, rather a brave and liberating envoi. Everywhere in this poet's world 'there's that buzz under everything' ('Open-eyed'). On all sides, as another poem's title announces, there is 'something going on'. The injunction of the whole collection is: Attend, pay attention! He asks of himself and of us what Lawrence's writing demands and excites: 'a new effort of attention'. Earlier in the collection there's a poem called 'Meanwhile' which attends to what is going on however well or badly we humans are living: the cycle of the seasons, the resurgence of plants and birdsong

Whether they know it, admit it, or not, human beings, some oftener than others, want things said.

(and a special commendation of the wren that 'in the dark short days had never stopped'). Bede's 'meanwhile' is a short life between two cold darknesses lived in the hope of heaven and the fear of hell. John Foggin's is the life lived here and now, fully attending – which entails attending also to how well or badly we treat one another and the planet on which the lives of all of us and of our children and their children depend.

The essence of the Anthropocene catastrophe is our careless or criminal harming of the web of earth's life and our ever faster detaching ourselves from it. In *Pressed for Time* there's a continual undertone of more or less oblique warnings of what will surely happen if we don't thoroughly mend our ways. The child believed the fires of Hell were in a disused pit under local fields ('Strata'); the adult recalls children and their 'glow-worm helmet lamps' lost underground 'Constant'). A sequence of poems is a roll-call of the most terrible mining disasters: Aberfan, Hartley, Senghenydd, Lofthouse … These were not in their day thought of as harbingers of fatal climate change, but the harvest itself, coal, in its own day harmful enough (the loss and stunting of countless lives, the fouling of the landscape) has put us increasingly at the mercy of fire and water, poisonous air and collapsing earth. The local observation 'The land sighs and sinks, and our houses/ all sit crank' ('Sapped') widens in its reference exponentially. The flat observation (in 'Buffalo Bill and the Miners') 'William Cody shot four thousand buffalo / in eighteen months' is a good instance of what we did back then and – variously applied – if we carry on doing it now, we are done for. As far as the plants and animals are concerned the Sixth Extinction is already well underway. Homo sapiens must be very dumb indeed not to realize their dying entails ours.

About the Author

David Constantine's publications include books of short stories from Comma Press and many translations and a *Collected Poems* from Bloodaxe.

REVIEWS

by: Roy Marshall, Tom Branfoot, Georgie Evans, Ian McMillan, Ian Pople , Belinda Cooke, Edmund Prestwich, Pam Thompson

ROY MARSHALL

Tony Hoagland, *Turn up the Ocean*, 85pp, £10.99
Bloodaxe Books.

Following **Tony Hoagland**'s death from cancer in 2018, his wife, the writer Kathleen Lee, went through his final, mostly unpublished poems, and assembled this collection. Those familiar with Hoagland will note that despite these poems being written during the last years of his illness, the dark sardonic humour for which he was known remains intact. The opening poem 'Bible All Out of Order' begins

One thing's for sure; in the future, the morgues are
        going to be full of tattoos. It's going to be
        more colourful and easier to manage;
"Hey Jeff, move Dolphin-Shoulder-Girl to tray seven."
"And get Mr.Flames-on-My-Neck out for the doc."

Hoagland's voice here has the pacy and colloquial quality of a stand-up comic. The reader's attention is caught with a scattering of seemingly unrelated images that the poet has challenged himself to make cohere. One of Hoagland's strengths is his ability to bring a poem full circle via various digressions. Like the best stand-ups, Hoagland isn't solely intent on shocking us or making us laugh. He wants to make us think and feel, to tear away at the (often) banal fabric of life until the bizarre, surreal, absurd and beautiful nature of our temporary and illusory existence is revealed. Typically, the poem travels from the dryly self-depreciating first person - 'my doctor asks what my symptoms are, I tell her / self-pity and a desire to apologize' and continues at speed through rich and varied cultural references. The heartbroken student from the film 'To Sir with Love' appears together with Cain and Abel, and references to an Italian tabloid story. Miraculously, given the bumpiness of the ride, the ultimate destination of this poem, and of many of the poems in this collection, is often a place of celebration, wonder and gratitude. In this instance Hoagland ends on a description of life as 'a blithering whirlwind of wonder'. Here we have the juxtaposition of 'blithering', suggesting perhaps the senseless and utterly hopeless nature of our human existence, with 'wonder'.

'Gorgon' bluntly presents a heart-breaking truth that many would find difficult to state openly; namely that 'the human family has turned out to be a conspiracy against / the planet'. Surprisingly, given the bleakness of this statement, it is hard not to emerge at the other side of the poem without feeling stronger. In dispensing with comforting platitudes, in looking directly at his subjects and stating what he perceives to be the harsh reality of the situation, Hoagland also tells himself and us that life is still worth living; that our 'job' is to live as fully aware creatures who continue to feel and notice, to 'stay calm. / Your job is to watch and take notes, / to go on looking.'

Anything else, complacency, acceptance or paralysis brought on by despair, would be a lost opportunity and perhaps an abdication of what Hoagland has decided is our 'job', to acknowledge and record both the horror and the beauty of all that we are part of.
In Powell and Pressburger's 1946 film, 'A Matter of Life and Death', David Niven, playing the pilot of a stricken aircraft, speaks to a young woman over the radio. As the fire rages and the wind howls through

Like the best stand-ups, Hoagland isn't solely intent on shocking us or making us laugh. He wants to make us think and feel …

the shot-up cockpit of the falling plane, Niven's character says, "I love you, June, because you are life, and I am leaving you." It is impossible to read Turn Up the Ocean without being aware of the context in which the poems were written. Hoagland was nearing the time when he would leave his life and these are his last messages.

Hoagland emerged in the nineties when much new American poetry seemed to be inspired by a combination of the confessional, Beat and New York schools. One of the main characteristics of this new school was its use of ironic playfulness and an awareness of language as an unstable, untrustworthy substance. Collectively, they demonstrated that language was ill-equipped to deal with abstracts such as truth or wisdom, whilst questioning any attempt to address whether those abstracts were plausible or desirable.

What set Hoagland apart was his apparent concern for expressing loyalty to his lived experience. In these, his last poems, Hoagland can be seen to be transitioning through various stages of grief, denial, anger, bargaining, depression, and acceptance. As psychologists have identified, these stages do not necessarily proceed in sequence, and this results in shifts in tone ranging from the apparently flippant to the profoundly meditative. This collection differs from his previous work in its occasional expressions of tenderness, vulnerability, and acknowledgement of frailty and sadness. In addition, a surprising and uplifting dimension is brought about by a sense of celebration of what he is leaving.

Apart from his celebrated sense of irony and wit, Hoagland's other strengths, linguistic awareness, dexterity with line breaks and sense of form, enabled him to let metaphorical and literal light into poems that deal with the darkest of subjects. A line is often allowed to float in a sea of white space so that its message is 'buoyed up'. This use of the page also allows a respectful, quiet distancing, enabling weighty subjects the space in which to be properly observed and absorbed.

This isn't an easy ride. In many of these poems Hoagland is still raging against the society he is part of. 'Well, what the fuck did you expect?' So, begins

'The reason he brought his gun to school; a Blues', a poem condemning the way the child in question has been 'socialised' by a rampantly consumerist system.

> The breast milk he drank was Coca-Cola
> and his balls
> were some of those Styrofoam peanuts
> that come as packing material in boxes for
> catalogue shopping.

The list continues, detailing the formative conditions that served to alienate a child. After this catalogue of horrors, and in the light of American's unfathomable position on gun control, it seems the opening line contains an entirely valid question.

Hoagland doesn't absolve himself from the culture he criticizes. Nor does he present a version of himself that might pass external or internal moral scrutiny. In 'Squad Car Light' there is a palpable sense of guilt at the speaker's privilege and avoidance of justice (or injustice) as visited on those who are less fortunate. As a neighbour is arrested (we are not told why) and led away, Hoagland thinks of the arrival of the Roman soldiers at Gethsemane, and of all those around the world who, unlike him, are 'putting their wrists behind their backs' in order to receive handcuffs.

Considering the circumstances in which they were written, it might be unreasonable to expect all the poems in this eighty-page collection to be of a consistently high standard. Hoagland was known to be a poet who constantly reworked his poems, both published and unpublished, and some of these pieces feel as though they would have benefited from further attention. A few have an unpolished feel, much like a set of demo tapes would sound when compared to a finished studio album. This does not make them any less compelling or moving, and in some instances the rawness and rough edges may be part of the appeal. There is a certain messiness to some of the work, as if a cascade of ideas and images have refused to be neatly tidied and boxed, as if this is a reflection of the fact that certainties and neatness are luxuries this poet

In these, his last poems, Hoagland can be seen to be transitioning through various stages of grief, denial, anger, bargaining, depression, and acceptance.

can no longer afford.

'Sunday at The Mall', its banal title contrasting starkly with its shocking content, has something of this raw, unpolished feel.

> Sweetheart, if I suddenly flop over in the
>   mall one afternoon
> while taking my old-person style exercise
> ... my teeth chattering like castanets,
> and my skull is going nok nonk nok on the
>   terracotta tiles
> of the well-swept mall floor.

The main point Hoagland, goes on to write, is *don't worry don't worry don't worry*. It is hard to imagine this poem offering any kind of solace or reassurance, but then it feels inappropriate to analyse what is essentially a love poem of excruciating openness.

If there is an element of sentimentality in some of these poems, (and why shouldn't there be?) there is also a palpable sense of struggle, a sense of regret for what will be lost. Alongside valiant attempts to accept loss with grace, Hoagland's voice is often tired, impatient, irascible. This is nothing new for a poet who didn't have much time for bullshit and artifice before he became terminally ill, and more than ever he stands before us naked, or at least in his underwear, endearingly open to exposing some of his own frailties and failings.

In a reflection on the poem 'The Definitive Journey' by Juan Ramon Jimenez, John Burnside writes that together with regret there is also "a sense of stoical celebration, a hymn to the continuity of life that, even as it persists, does not include the celebrant." This seems an entirely fitting description of what is happening in many of the poems in *Turn Up the Ocean*. Continuity is symbolised by the wren which appears both in the last poem in the collection, 'Peaceful Transition' and the (typically) fabulously titled 'On Why I Must Decline to Receive The Prayers You Say You Are Constantly Sending.' Note the casually sceptical tone, 'you say you are sending.' And what a stroke of brilliance, to call the diminutive bird 'big', embodying as she does in this poem, the vast and unfathomable mystery, persistence and fortitude of the natural world.

In the somewhat less fabulously titled 'Nature is Strong' Hoagland drops all his wry humour and cynicism to celebrate this resilience.

> After the nine species of moth
> that carried a fine yellow pollen from
>   one vine to the next
> at the edge of the forest in Belize-
> after all nine species have been declared extinct,
> a tenth species will appear.

In Hoagland's exploration of grief and pain there is gratitude for friendship (in the touching 'Landscape Without Jason') and for beauty, which can arise and be celebrated anywhere, even in the most unlikely circumstances.

> There was a beautiful silence in the house,
> when my mother was dying in the spring
>   ('Immersion')

This quiet poem would be affecting even if it were not so profoundly linked to the poet's knowledge of his own impending death.

Despite moments of tranquillity, there are no neat resolutions in this collection, to the reality of dying. Life remains absurd, tragic, painful and beautiful, but ultimately better than the alternative. The voice in many of these poems is one of a frail, impassioned, imperfect, frustrated, mystified and loving human being who remains deeply engaged in trying to name the sources of suffering, both his own and that of the world, and in examining them from multiple perspectives. 'Success', among other things, is an expression of regret at lack of focus and care.

> Did you carry (your life) carefully, like a
>   brimful cup of water,
> bound for a particular flower?

Despite moments of tranquillity, there are no neat resolutions in this collection, to the reality of dying.

Or did you keep accidentally turning around
to look at something else,
and slosh it all over the place, like me?

There are many moments of self-reproach, but on a more hopeful note, the observable world, particularly the natural world, acts as a kind of antidepressant or pain reliever. For Hoagland, to look closely is to lose self-importance, to escape what he described in an interview as "the bottomless implosion of subjectivity and psychology." The harrowing 'Bandage' allows him an opportunity to bring his lived experience close enough to own it.

Down in the pocket of this old green pair of pants

I find a dirty, wadded-up bandage
with a rusty coin-sized stain in the cotton pad,

hidden where I showed it during one of those days
when I was going to the clinic every few weeks
getting a bag of steroids and gemcitabine

pumped though the tip of a needle

The examination of pain in these poems feels like an act of generosity. The shafts of light, hope, humour and encouragement that run through the darkness seem like acts of kindness. *Turn Up the Ocean* is Hoagland's parting gift, and I am glad to be among its grateful recipients.

About the Author

Roy Marshall's publications include *The Sun Bathers* and a book of translations *After Montale* (both from Shoestring).

TOM BRANFOOT

Lila Matsumoto, *Two Twin Pipes Sprout Water*, 88pp, £8, Prototype, 2021

Jane Burn, *Be Feared*, 72pp, £9.99, Nine Arches Press, 2021.

These divergent collections find common ground in weirding the mundane. **Lila Matsumoto**'s *Two Twin Pipes Sprout Water* arrives as a typography and design-oriented book-object. Prototype's manifesto is that, 'Each publication is unique in its form and presentation, and the aesthetic of each object is considered critical to its production'. Constructed from five discrete sequences, 'Pictorial Programme' opens with prose poems of pandemic surrealism interlaced with climate anxiety: 'All around / us was casual destruction, and I don't blame it on the weather'; 'His apples were sour but /the news shouldn't have been, because no doubt anywhere we are, / someone has died there'. Matsumoto's irreverent and absurd approach to poetics is clear from the outset:

[...] Later the conference
organiser's car was found being scratched up by a
peacock which
had seen its own reflection in the bonnet

An allegiance to medievalism unravels throughout the text, most parodically in 'Fiefdom of x', where each page is ornamented with a drop cap and presbyopic font size. Her brocaded tableau vivant of the Middle Ages is undercut with humour; characters donning 'Phrygian caps and cross-gartered yellow and red stockings' are 'engaged in a post-industry folk disco'. Matsumoto's language is carnivalesque and playfully arcane, 'Across three large arcades on / the cope's spine, a plaintive stream blips in / a lingy moor'.

'Rouleau of songs' is the closest we get to lyric, though crucially experimental, animated with vivid lines: 'Cloth is lighter where the sun baffles its border'; 'A litany of things inessential'; 'The city is a body ringing itself with sound'. 'By likeness' evokes gustatory displeasure, 'Music is flesh juice' we're told in abject factuality, before the command to 'Human yourself better!'.

Marking the collection as an interdisciplinary text,

Matsumoto's irreverent and absurd approach to poetics is clear from the outset ...

'EyeBread' features charcoal drawings by Esme Armour and a remarkable epigraph from Esther Leslie about life being constituted from 'tiny events and encounters'. Leslie's comments about infinitesimal events grant existential significance to the diaristic form with entries such as 'Tuesday, mouldy as an abducted mushroom', complete with the cryptic emblem of a buckled bench with the text 'Abducted Mushroom'. Finding correlation between the image and text becomes less important than enjoying the dissonance, particularly with the image of Madonna and Child captioned 'A Favourite Snack'.

The final section, 'Evening fast out the window' contains concise poems operating like flash fiction with the elliptical tone of German expressionism. Condensed and pared back - with the exception of 'Trombone', a fable in which the moral is elusive - these poems thrum with potential, there is something gnostic beyond them.

Be Feared, **Jane Burn**'s most recent collection, is an unstoppable force of fierce imagery. One of her strengths is the revivification of outmoded forms fitted with entrancing titles: 'Coronach for my slender waist'; 'Thumbelina's Birth as Told in the Style of Gregorian Chant'; and the masterful 'Villanelle to Cold Psalms'. The latter features this haunting tercet:

I bear a ghost of gloom in the curl of my palm.
I am the moonlight's gash where the sky is torn.
I imagine the dead I would make in the strange of
your arms.

Throughout her collection, the lyric 'I' is assured and resilient to histories of hostility and oppression. As it progresses, the titular phrase transforms from feeling unsafe, in 'This is a Frankenstein Night':

[...] Be feared that someone
might grab your back, pull out your lungs, crack
your spine,
ground you like a broken doll

to a phoenix-like imperative, *be* feared.

Burn locates herself in the feminist mythological revisionist territory of Sexton, Plath, and Duffy with her rewritings of fairy tales such as *Snow White* and *The Snow Queen*. This collection of lyrics approaches themes of motherhood, neurodivergence, sexuality, and nature. Her imagery is most considered when describing the natural world, as the river 'rolled a wet hymn across feral land':

I saw the grey priest of a heron
fly overhead like a slow angel   bearing the crucifixion
of its splinter feet

Care for the other-than-human illuminates her utterances. Certain poems, such as 'Magic Mirror', are almost too decorative in their language use and risk feeling like 'messy devotions', to quote her poem, 'Look at me, lingering outside this murdered church'. Burn's attentiveness to the magick of language sometimes yields verbosity. A rhetorical device which both services and disservices Burn's poetry is anthimeria, using one part of speech as another, as in 'a mystery of worms'; 'devotion of swans'; 'shamble of hair'. Certain uses are electric, however, 'where a chestnut horse walks beneath the sun / like a bonfire of muscle'.

Domestic scenes are shot through with holy light, piled 'plates like holy disks' and 'shrouds of vacant clothes' litter the surroundings. These environments stage interventions in neurodivergent subjectivity,

when my husband tried to get into bed with me
I screamed [...]

                              because I had everything arranged
and he made it un-arranged

Burn represents the disarray and confusion of autism through the ordinariness which defines the domestic lyric, so critical to feminist poetics. Devotion to the weird divinity of language is the common denominator of Burn and Matsumoto in their respective projects.

Burn locates herself in the feminist mythological revisionist territory of Sexton, Plath, and Duffy with her rewritings of fairy tales such as Snow White *and* The Snow Queen.

About the Author

Tom Branfoot is a winner of The New Poets Prize featured in this issue (p76)

GEORGIE EVANS

Caroline Bird, *Rookie: Selected Poems*, 192pp, £11.69,
Carcanet Press, 2022

babe grab a
coat, zip up, storm's coming.

Those are the lines I read before the pan boils over and I have to stand on a chair and flap a tea towel furiously at the smoke alarm. A minute later, the pans are cooling off, the windows open. I pick up the book I'd thrown aside in panic. It's Caroline Bird, *Rookie: Selected Poems*.

Since *Rookie* arrived at my flat I've been in the habit of picking out random poems and reading them while I cook tea. And I've realised poetry is very well-suited to the task: I'll read a poem, get up to stir a sauce or turn something over in the oven, then sit and read another while everything cooks some more.

This poem, "Run", I've paired with spaghetti, but it might have been better as a complement to a tasty yet weird-looking soup; the poem's first lines — 'If my language was water / it would be rainwater' — are tricky to see past when I'm trying to compare it to food. But the poem is a smart play on this idea, that language can be wet, that it can become muddy and sticky or it can glitter and soothe. My favourite part is the counter to all this, which comes at the end:

If my silence was water

I'd be heading for you, top
news bulletin, forecast

world over: babe grab a
coat, zip up, storm's coming.

Then there I am, burning everything, smoke alarm. It's oddly fitting. My poem-food combinations haven't paired so well on other nights, unfortunately, but I'm still interested in what Bird's poetry can throw my way

when I don't expect it. There's the night I eat out of Tupperware in the back seat of my mum's car, reading a poem I've seen Bird perform, called "The Ground". The conceit of this poem is that every time the speaker thinks they've finished falling, they haven't; they keep tumbling towards new, lower grounds. Even though I know the poem, every employment of that conceit was like driving over a pothole. You think she's finished, and she pulls you that bit further. It's daring. (As is eating lentil stew in the back of the car.)

There's another night I come home hungry, the pub's drinks having their effect, and I'm swaying as I reheat daal. I start to read the poems aloud. They echo, and it's as if I've been read *and* been read to. I think proudly, It's the kind of thing one of Bird's speakers would notice.

All this folds together to forge in me a link between poetry and meals, in which writing becomes a thing not unlike cooking, and words begin to smell the way ingredients do before they are brought together.

The main ingredient in Bird's poems is, easily, surprise. In poetry I think it is the most difficult thing, because the poet has to invent this bubble of surprise, fix it in, perhaps cover it up a little so it's not so obvious, and then continue to play the part of the speaker as if they didn't know what was about to happen. It's like throwing a football at your own head and not screwing up your face in anticipation of the blow. But this poet can do it: it's what she's doing in "The Ground", and in another poem, "The Deadness", where the first lines are:

It's like being a windmill in a vacuum
packed village. Weekends are the worst.

— and the last lines are:

but the air hasn't moved in months, either
we're living in separate weathers
or you have fake snow on your coat.

This is what you come to anticipate: Bird's line breaks are like the extra step on the staircase. The poems' speakers give you a pair of glasses, you put

Since Rookie *arrived at my flat I've been in the habit of picking out random poems and reading them while I cook tea.*

them on, and suddenly you're upside-down or you're seeing double or everything around you has halved in size and is singing. Bird can alchemise the world and, somehow, she still makes it familiar.

If surprise is the bread of Bird's poetry, then personality is the butter. *Rookie* fizzes with all these little characters; they're confused, sweet, tired, loving. I'm sure none of the poems' speakers would call themselves Caroline, though they're so real they must have been instilled with varying amounts of the poet's real thoughts and fears. So many of the poems in *Rookie* could be described as love poems — not in a *shall-I-compare-thee* way, rather a startled, whirlwind-y way — that this could only be the work of someone who enjoys love: loving people, loving language, loving fun.

Although love isn't always easy for *Rookie*'s speakers: in the poem "A Love Song", Divorce becomes a lodger that a couple decides to butter up 'like a treasured child'. In "Bow Your Head and Cry", a couple's love dies on a cobbled street; only the speaker, not their partner, is there to hold love's hand as it passes.

I finish *Rookie* on a night I can't be bothered cooking. In the last poem, "Speechless", the words feel the same: 'vowels crammed like backpacks, their lettered / backs are broken from it / syllables bent from all the shoulder-ing / but tonight all the words left'. They're wrung out, politely saying, 'No, thank you.' No one could blame them. They've done a good job. I leave the book how I'd like best to leave a meal: satisfied, slightly drunk, and thinking I'd happily devour it again tomorrow.

About the Author

Georgie Evans is a writer and bookseller from Halifax. She is currently working on a novel about deafness and dementia.

IAN McMILLAN

Imogen Foster, *The Grass Boat*, £6.00, Mariscat Press

Ellen Renton, *An Eye For An Eye For An Eye*, £5.99, Stewed Rhubarb Press

Helen Quah, *Dog Woman*, £7.00, Out-Spoken Press

Genevieve Carver, *Landsick*, £8.99, Broken Sleep Books

I've said it before and I'll say it again: Pamphlets are the engine room of the poetry scene. They're the printed equivalent of the open mic night or the DIY single or the pop-up gig in the abandoned house and without them the literary world would be less approachable, less democratic, less gloriously cacophonous.

Here, then, are four very different and fairly recent pamphlets for us all to get our teeth into from four very different and very worthwhile presses.

Imogen Foster, published by Mariscat Press, that jewel in the Scottish poetry crown, offers us work constructed with a deep and fertile combination of craft and heart, which is like a combination of craft and art but more so. Her work gleams with precise observation couched in rhythms that nudge you into understanding and a kind of shared memory:

I see my Grandpa, the dry,
Pencil-shaving sweat-scent
Of his flannel shirt, his fingers
Contracted into claws, unable
To grasp a tool's handle.

I really like the work the commas do in that stanza, slowing us down and mirroring Grandpa's slowing down, and I like the subtle chiming of unable and han-dle. The poems here do that easier-said-than-done job of showing us familiar things and places and making them unfamiliar: ice cream, buses, teeth, bugs. Imogen Foster makes me want to look and listen harder, and that has to be a good thing.

Ellen Renton is a poet and theatre maker and performer who has a visual impairment and whose work is at home both on the page and in the air and in the intersection between the two:

The poems here do that easier-said-than-done job of showing us familiar things and places and making them unfamiliar ...

Do you pull morning
Tight around yourself
Like a coat
Or does it wear you?

She writes in 'How Far Can You See?', the line endings helping us along the poem's contours, the rhythms helping us into the poem's ideas. Renton's images can startle the reader/listener and encourage us to read/listen more closely. In Boomerang, for instance:

Without my glasses
The bath looks twice

Its length   The taps might
As well be Inchcolm
And Inchgarvie lost under haar

Inchcolm and Inchgarvie being two islands in The Firth of Forth that have never before, I think I can say with confidence, been compared to taps, and now can never be uncompared to taps. Refreshing language is one of a poet's main jobs, I reckon, and Ellen Renton does it wonderfully well creating new places for words to dance in:

each time I'm almost surprised
by what the morning looks like but
not quite
today it woke me speechless
now I've got my tongue back

which is from Contact, a beautifully descriptive and philosophical poem about sight and lack of it, and contact lenses and the language we use.

Helen Quah, in Dog Women, has a sequence of poems scattered throughout the pamphlet called 'When I Marry A White Man' which convey a kind of intimacy and distance at the same time:

When we enter our hotel room
my husband puts the receiver

on the table and keeps his shoes on.
The room smells burnt like carpet
has the stale colours of old sitcoms.
        (When I Marry A White Man) II

        And

I'm made of stains and hiccups.
there are old honeymoon photos
sunk into the top shelf of our marriage
        (When I Marry A White Man) III

        And

When the house is quiet
and I've emptied all kindness
from its fact – I'll touch a face
in the wet mirror. Pour over
my worn slab half myself awake
more brutal than before.
        (When I Marry A White Man) IV

These poems, it seems to me, are the backbone of the pamphlet and they underline Quah's mastery of language, her way of wrongfooting the reader in a good way, leading them up a garden path of meaning and sense, as in the last two lines of that final piece where the words seem to melt into each other and seem to glow with a querulous light. Each line, each image, each selection of where to end the line and the stanza seem to make each of the poems here more striking, more unusual, more thoughtful and surprising.

then a van turns a corner all over my dress
                my head dilating
                        in the rear view mirror.
        (Self)

In *Landsick* Genevieve Carver takes us to the coast, to shores that are at once literal and metaphorical. My spellcheck didn't like Landsick, which is the mark of a newly-coined word, and much of the pamphlet brims

Refreshing language is one of a poet's main jobs, I reckon, and Ellen Renton does it wonderfully well creating new places for words to dance in ...

124

with new coinings of meaning and observation:

I combed the nooks of Ravenscar
where seals haul out on rocks
like turkey breasts on stainless worktops.
  ('The Selkie Searches for Her Skin')

'I'm drowning,' I say, stitching you into the hem
                                        of my jeans
and dragging you under, sinking us right down
through the floorboards, all the way
to the bottom of the deep blue sea.
  ('Blue Monday')

Carver works hard to make each line do each poem's heavy lifting, but the hard work is never obvious and the heavy lifting is only performative when it needs to be; these are poems of place and poems of nature but with humanity and empathy at their heart.

All four of these pamphlets are well worth reading and all these publishers need our support. After all, without them the poetry train would just be a poetry rail replacement bus, and that would be no fun.

About the Author

Ian McMillan's books include the memoir *My Sand Life, My Pebble Life* (Adlard Coles) and *To Fold the Evening Star: New & Selected Poems* (Carcanet)

IAN POPLE

Carola Luther, *On the Way to Jerusalem Farm*, £11.99, Carcanet Press

Stephen Payne, *The Wax Argument & other thought experiments* and *The Windmill Proof*, £6.00 and £10.00, Happen*Stance* Press

Ruth Sharman, *Rain Tree*, £10.00, Templar Poetry

The title of **Carola Luther**'s third book for Carcanet gives some idea of the trajectory of the poems inside. In part, we are on a pilgrimage and in part a secular journey; the object of which is a kind of Jerusalem. And Jerusalem has always been a contested destination. Not only is it religiously contested between Jew, Christian and Muslim, but religious context has always led to political contest; a political contest that started even before the Crusades. There is also a sense of variousness held in the third term in the title, the word, 'farm.'

What that title might also indicate is the power of Luther's writing. That power is announced in the first sequence of the book, 'Letters to Rasool.' The titles of the individual poems have a slightly rhetorical, inclusive feel to them, for example, 'On Flight,' 'On Faith,' 'On Despair.' Each poem speaks to the Rasool of the sequence title, though we don't really know who Rasool finally is. Thus, the poems are a dialogue to which the reader is an audience. However, the interactions between the narrator and Rasool are given with such detail that the reader quickly becomes part of the intimacy of the exchange. The poems are set out in a typographic open form which is difficult to reproduce in a review. But that open form is also part of the dialogue and the intimacy. This is because the open form so skilfully deployed by Luther not only pulls the reader in, but also holds and stages the surrounding text.

The dialogue flirts with a kind of surrealism. 'On Giants' starts, 'Last week I lost the map Rasool / Seaside people helped me search the sand / A woman whistled *Molly Malone sweet Molly Malone* / and I returned to that pale morning // You and I / balanced / on basalt columns / pretending to be giants / yelling / *alive alive oh* / to our stone twins / over the sea' The lack of punctuation combines with the positioning of the words to create a particular rhythm. And the sense of the fantastic in the events described is linked to an almost bathetic normalcy; the seaside people who help the search, the woman whistling, the childlike balancing

In part, we are on a pilgrimage and in part a secular journey; the object of which is a kind of Jerusalem.

on the columns. Luther offers fantasy anchored in the everyday.

Luther, who lives in the Calder Valley in Northern England, also writes beautifully about that part of the world. Its landscape is often harsh and demanding, but when the sun emerges it is rich and involving, too. In 'Slipping of Light', the first poem in a section entitled, 'Herd', Luther comments that the sun 'seems / to feel its way, igniting torches stored inside / sheep, birds, trees, the hill, so they might be / their own lamps. This, I believe, is similar to love.' This is the imbued world, a world that might be even more than itself. That imbuing fills the surrealism of the 'Letters to Rasool.' In this section of the book though Luther reaches into the natural world. And that reach culminates in the lovely, simple declaration that ends the poem.

Elsewhere, the connection with the spiritual is made more explicit. Luther has a poignant elegy for the poet, Mark Hinchliffe, 'Poetry Reading 14 November 2019.' Luther imagines Hinchliffe's spirit attending a poetry reading. At the end of the poem, the spirit lifts its 'head, seem[s] to / see all the souls amongst us, your eyes have changed, / deep yellow now, the colour of November / beech leaves bright with rain –. ' This shows the searching empathy that Luther has. As we have seen, such empathy is in a surrealism anchored in reality; the depictions of the natural world embody love, and that personal empathy with those she is close to shown throughout this involving book.

Stephen Payne has two recent collections from Happenstance. The first of these is a book length collection *The Windmill Proof* from 2021 and the second a pamphlet from 2022, *the Wax Argument and Other thought experiments*. Payne is an emeritus professor of Computer Science and conducted research in cognitive science and human-computer interaction. And the connection between poet and profession is clear throughout these two collections. In *The Windmill Proof*, poems about, ostensibly, mathematical or scientific situations are interleaved with poems that take their subject from much more personal, human motifs. Not that Payne's poems about maths are without their

human dimension. The poem 'Triangle' begins, 'The geometer said / *Let trigons be trigons* / but 'triangle' it stays // for pointy polygon,' and ends 'so if Alex loves Blake and Blake loves Chris / it would be easier / if Alex loves Chris.' These quotations show part of Payne's method. There is the 'mathematical' set-up, whose potential seriousness and, perhaps, dryness, Payne subverts with neat humour. Then there is the ending in which the 'triangulation' of a relationship, and the seriousness of that, is both emphasised but also subverted by the references to characters from *Dynasty*. And there are other geometrical punnings and 'triangulations' in Payne's collection, in, for example, the poem 'Square' which ends, 'Like Berkeley Square / where the nightingale sang.'

That kind of light 'scientific' verse might become a little one-dimensional if it were Payne's only technique, successful as it is. However, the other 'human' poems show how Payne's empirical eye is also empathetic. In the short sequence, 'Walking in São Carlos', the narrator walks around the Brazilian city of that name and observes small, human scenes in those streets. In 'Avenida Dr Carlos Botelho', Payne depicts three dogs 'riding on the back / of a battered pickup truck.' The dogs bark at everything up to and including, 'At the juggler on the crossroad, the arc / of hic clubs, his golden arms, they bark.' Here Payne becomes a Martian poet, describing the policeman directing traffic at the crossroad as a 'juggler.'

Payne's 2022 pamphlet *The Wax Argument & other thought experiments* takes this melding of the scientific and the human further. Payne comments that the poems 'are based on philosophical thought experiments.' He also states that the poems in the pamphlet 'observe traditional forms.' Thus, Payne has set himself two quite strenuous formal problems; the melding of thought experiment and poetic forms. The result is a small gem, whose success is because Payne's imagination creates an absorbing middle way between the 'thought experiment', and the form the poem inhabits. The resultant poems are a little scenario in which the thought experiment is reimagined.

Payne is an emeritus professor of Computer Science and conducted research in cognitive science and human-computer interaction. And the connection between poet and profession is clear …

Such poems are slightly more 'serious' than some of Payne's other writing; a seriousness because Payne not only takes the thought experiment seriously but is intent on reimagining its human consequences. In 'A Mother-in-law learns to love her daughter-in-law', for example, based on Iris Murdoch's book *the Idea of Perfection*, Payne writes, 'All M had needed, she came to realise, / was the occasion and the mental space / to reappraise / her memories of D- / those gestures and responses, jokes and moans- / to acknowledge and resolve their ambiguity.' Although the language is formal and Latinate, Payne underpins that formality with the poignancy of human interaction.

Ruth Sharman achieves a difficult triangulation between nostalgia, memory and the needs of the present. Sharman's third book, *Rain Tree*, contains poems based upon her revisiting the India and in particular, the Chennai of her birth and first six years. The emotional tone for the book is set with the epigraph from Bash , 'Even in Kyoto / hearing the cuckoo calling / I long for Kyoto.' Early in the collection, in the poem that records Sharman's 'Arriving in Chennai,' the question that she repeats is, 'What am I doing ...?' Elsewhere she answers that question with 'I'm searching for reminders / written in the landscape, as if the past were still present / but the writing hard to read,' ('Tamil Nadu'). Sharman's skill is to evoke both past and present so precisely that we share in the emotions that these details arouse.

The past is the one that Sharman and her parents shared in her early years in Chennai. In 'Untitled,' Sharman imagines her father, 'nipping over these rocks / with [his] net, then heading / for the far ridge, drawn / by that intensity of green.' Sharman portrays her father in the pursuit of butterflies. The father's almost obsession with butterflies and the ways that his daughter connects with that has echoed through Sharman's work from her first volume *The Birth of the Owl Butterflies*

The sheer sensuality of Sharman's writing convinces. Many of the scenes that she describes might be described as 'exotic' to the casual reader, but what grips is her searching involvement. In part, as we have seen that involvement comes from Sharman's history and her need to understand that history anew. But the details are so clearly written that it is difficult for the reader to stand aside. In the quotation above, the phrase 'drawn by that intensity of green,' offers a kind of mimesis whereby the reader is also drawn into that intense green.

In 'Breaking In,' she describes breaking into the house in which she lived as a child. This house had been left intact after it was turned into company offices. The result of the breaking in is, however, to throw up further questions, 'What is the meaning of all / these small windowless rooms / and why are the stairs right here? / Is this where I spat spinach / into my napkin? Is this where / our parents slept, this space / littered with papers and files / like debris in the aftermath of a quake? / Was this tiny room really mine?' In part, these are questions that we might all ask on returning to that kind of scene. But Sharman's questions have a personal definition and purpose.

Sensuality is present throughout Sharman's explorations of India. Her gaze misses little, as in 'Glimpse' in which Sharman sees a woman leaving a holy man, 'framed in the doorway / in her garland of marigolds, / the white scarf, her dress / patterned with blue betel leaves.' Or in the poem 'Annabel promised me a snake-bird ...', where Sharman observes 'the couple sitting on a veranda after dark, / he in his white lungi, she leaning forward, / bare-armed, to adjust the lamp.' And with this gaze are the quiet felicities that convince us that Sharman has really seen: the details of the dress in 'Glimpse', the 'bare-armed' in 'Annabel...'

Rain Tree formidably adumbrates the way the self is in transit between past and present, between the child's place in the family, and the adult's gaze on that child, between the self in and of one culture, and the way the self finds itself in another culture whilst not of that culture.

The sheer sensuality of Sharman's writing convinces.

About the Author

Ian Pople's *Spillway: New and Selected Poems* is published by Carcanet.

127

BELINDA COOKE

Marija Kneževic, *Breathing Technique*, trans. Sibelan Forrester, £10.99, 203pp, Zephyr Press, 2020.

Geovanni Pascoli, *Selected Poems*, trans. Taije Silverman with Marina Della Putta Johnston, 179pp, £16.99, Princeton Univ. Press, 2019

Eugenio Montale, *After Montale*, trans. Roy Marshall, 27pp, £7.50, Shoestring Press, 2019

The Serbian poet, **Marija Kneževic's** *Breathing Technique* offers a mix of personal spirituality ('To be actually never. / To be now. / Singularity in passage.' ('The beginning of cartography')) and cynicism about contemporary ills: ('We're a litter of childhood diseases. / And everything we touch starts whimpering.' ('The Landless')). World weariness and transcendental wonder are caught, here, particularly in the final line's plain diction:

Everything that's hers is in her.
She is her own border.
Besides flowing, she has no other dimensions.
...
Close as a touch and simultaneously
who knows where.
She has already arrived everywhere.
　　('The River's name')

Combining these conflicting emotions makes for her distinctive voice with the the city and geography as the backdrop to her scrutiny of consumerism, war, economic and political displacement.

Generally, human warmth and a universal spirituality do repeatedly come out on top: 'To be kin. To anyone' ('The beginning of cartography'); here in an out of body experience: 'I, trapped by time's slow flow, Lived a whole somnambulistic omnibus' ('Anaesthesia') and in her belief that the dead remain with us:

'When I die,

you must be sure to leave the window open.
...
When you think I'm not there,
if you don't question the origins
of my requests,

I'll love you more
than the living.
　　('The last lecture on tenderness')

And even when moving to darker themes, she remains tolerant of human frailty: 'People are good. / As much as they can be' ('The season of good people'), even while remaining cynical on the naïve idealism of the young: 'the empty desire of their own song.' ('Open after midnight')

But nevertheless, people in the city are constantly under threat, a fact she captures with pithy aphoristic phrases: 'I have fear for this city / Ever since love left fo a distant convalescence' (Surrender of the city'); 'The city where all this happened / was showing signs of life / in all the wrong places' ('A diary of minor troubles'), 'The way the street understands loneliness // can't even be imagined' ('Fado triste'); She can also be darkly humourous, here speaking to the dispossessed: asylum seekers ('They unloaded us onto this land / And commanded: You're free.' ('Cargo))

Her poem 'Day' shows her skill with the observational poem where yet another city poem starts with the day-to-day with a woman simply digging her town plot, but we are then taking into the mother's concerns for her absent addict daughter and then further to the universal parental concerns:

While her fingers undermine the wall of worry
While apparently planting flowers,
She sees young soldiers in the deserts of Asia,
Little girls half naked, almost blind
Under layers of makeup fading, similar –
As if she had given birth to them all.

Such lines strongly point to her ability to act as public

Combining these conflicting emotions makes for her distinctive voice with the the city and geography ...

voice as well as a deeply reflective one. From this collection, it is not hard to see why Kneževic is regarded as one of Serbia's most important writers, with the added luck of her translator Sibelan Forrester, who is spot on in capturing these shifting tones.

Giovanni Pascoli's (1855-1912) childhood was tragically cut short by his father's murder, the death of his mother and three siblings, leaving him to care for the remaining ones. In spite of this, his *Selected Poems* is a joyful collection with the self in harmony with the natural world, while death is a natural process:

> But, beneath the love,
> the deeper voice
> of a grave responds – as if
> to the song's true wish.
> ('Sunday Dawn')

Likewise, the past doesn't leave him bitter, but comforts him in the present: 'such sweetness reaches me here / from the infinite sweetness back then.' ('Back Then')

But, perhaps, the loss of a proper childhood was the trigger for him so often idealising nature, along with so many hyperbolic descriptions, which the reader will see as not real, but as nevertheless delightful also to indulge in. In 'Fides' (Latin for 'Faith') the sky is a gateway to an alternative fairytale forest world for a young child, painted in gleaming colours:

> When twilight glowed a rare, brilliant red
> and the cypress seemed gold, a gold dusting,
> the mother explained to her very small son
> that, up there, it's nothing but gardens.
> Her son is asleep and dreams of gold
> branches, trees made of gold, golden forests.
> Meanwhile, outside, in the blackness of night,
> the cypress weeps rain, and wars with the wind.

Elsewhere we have the kind of romanticised rural world with its panoramic shifts from large to small. The church bells symbolise unity between nature and man, before telesscoping down to the woman's face by the window. Note also the careful selection of concrete detail that makes her vivid to the reader, along with the poem's general emphasis on sound: 'murmurings', 'surge', 'scrape', 'rustle':

> The rosy belfry must have heard
> a thousand murmurings that day,
> a surge of urgent swallows to their nests.
>
> Now, in the quiet of the afternooon,
> I hear a chair scrape wood indoors, the rustle
> of a skirt, abrupt: a woman's gentle,
> puzzled face appears beside the window.
> ('That Day')

The focus on nature that dominates the whole of the collection becomes increasingly tethered to a search for meaning in his later poems, as in a number of specific animal poems: 'You look for a Truth. Your thought seems / an immense sea: in the sea's immensity, / a shell; in the shell, a pearl' ('Black Cat') and note here, the microscopically precise description of the ox's eyes combined with transforming the animals to something sacred:

> Enormous in the ox's eyes, the willow
> and the alder rise inside a flush
> of dusty light. Cows roam through grass
> like sacred cattle of a mythic past.
> ('The Ox')

Increasingly, poem after poem gives subtle sense of self as part of the universe:

> Still he turns pages, while shadows pull in
> and wind-swollen curtains, and carrying
> vacant constellations of stars,
>
> the sacred night arrives.
> ('The Book III')

All and all, this is a superb collection and one is struck

The focus on nature that dominates the whole of the collection becomes increasingly tethered to a search for meaning in his later poems ...

by the diverse ways he explores the natural world of seasons settings and wild life with numerous poems it would be great to quote in full. And one thing Princeton Press's Lockert library can always be relied upon is specialist translators who are passionate and expert about their subject matter with detailed introductions and thorough background notes. Here in this substantial volume they have done it again.

Roy Marshall's class translations of **Eugenio Montale's** (1896-1891) in *After Montale,* are far less endeared to life, dramatically contrasting Kneževic and Pascoli with his expressions of cold, bitter, existential angst:

> Don't ask me to place a frame round
> the human condition, to trace the soul's
> shapeless form, for a poem that will blaze
> like a crocus on a drought-struck lawn.

Marshall's introduction is helpful here. His attraction to the poetry was due to his own grandfather fighting against the fascists in World War One leading to a very personal choice: 'It often seemed as if the poems were choosing me.' From here he notes three poetic periods: early short lyrics of 'nihilistic modernism'; interwar ideological uncertainty and, finally, poems that mix 'deadpan humour' and a 'certain world weariness.' In the face of all of this, for Marshall, the resulting poems still provide comfort in the face of the reality that humanity will continue making the same mistakes.

Certainly, in places, bleakness is so extreme it is almost funny:

> Go out into the midday sun,
> downcast and stunned to feel
> life's nothing but a walk beside
> a wall topped with broken bottles.
> ('Midday')

Like a Pascoli alter ego, Montale also looks to the natural world but as a mystery that cannot unravelled:

> Leave the soporific reeds
> in their bed, come instead
> and watch life on its journey
>
> towards dust. Walk out into
> this haze, a glare that will
> make you feel weak.
>
> These clouded mountain tops
> are like us, hidden from ourselves
> and from others.
>
> The serentiy of the sky depends
> on only one certainy. Light.
> ('Light')

Of course, look beneath the surface and, perhaps this is Montale protesting too much, more a Hamlet-like disdain for humanity mixed with love of human mystery –'What a piece of work is a man... and yet,to me, what is this quintessence of dust?' – for there is still a certain wonder here, for example:

> From out of darkness bodies
> are drawn towards light. To merge
> and blend is the fate of everything.
>
> Bring me a sunflower to trace the sun's
> trajectory while its essence escape in haze;
> bring me a sunfower, its face ablaze.'
> ('Sunflower')

Like Pascoli also, he observes in microscopic detail, here with a shocking precision suggestion nature in the face of war:

> I've seen suffering
> in a choked stream, brittle veins
> on a parched leaf, in the eye of a fallen horse.
>
> But I've hardly ever seen
> its opposite. Only evidence

Like a Pascoli alter ego, Montale also looks to the natural world but as a mystery that cannot unravelled ...

of divine indifference; in the statues
of the soporific part, in a white cloud
and in the high-flying hawk.
    ('The Evidence')

For, the poet, in the end, bleakness is often empowering for poetry, line after line in these gems captures the way this is indeed Montale's subject matter: 'Words can mimic the wind … / But deeper truths exist in silence / where a sob is a song of peace.' ('Frown'). Life's only meaning lies in the living of it in all its uniqueness: 'Time never moulds a a sand dune / the same way twice.' ('Wind and Flags') and our job is just to keep on keeping on and now, like Kneževic, for Montale, the dead do in some way remain with us:

Kelp is dragged up

on the beach, but our lives refuse
such helpless indignity: the part of us
we thought had stopped, resigned to its limits,
somehow rages on, and the heart struggles
like a marsh hen, caught in the mesh
of one of those nets.

Maybe the dead
aren't at rest either; maybe a force
more pitiless than life
pulls them back to theose beaches.
Their shadow moves across
our memoirs, silent, formless,
close enough to brush our skin,
to remind us of their existence
before they're lost in the sea's sieve.
    ('The Dead')

About the Author

Belinda Cooke has published translations including the *Selected Poems of Marina Tsvetaeva* (Worple Press) and recently a full length collection of her own poems, *Stem* (High Windows Press).

EDMUND PRESTWICH

Sean O'Brien, *Embark*, 72pp, £10.99, Picador Poetry, 2022

Philip Gross, *The Thirteenth Angel*, 96pp, £12, Bloodaxe Books, 2022

Selima Hill, *Women in Comfortable Shoes*, 256pp, Bloodaxe Books, 2023

In *Embark*, Sean O'Brien deftly shifts between registers and tones to present and think about the world in different ways. In his elegies, melancholy recollection is expressed in a way that combines elegance with conversational intimacy. Other poems are more obviously highly wrought, like 'Of the Angel' with its archaic-sounding title. This describes a boy at a Remembrance Day ceremonial –

The poor mad angel boy of twelve
With the unblinking gold-green stare
And the frightening permanent smile

That should be love but cannot be
Is brought by his mother to join the crowd.

That opening already trembles between the mundane and the visionary. Compassion and the near-banality of line 5 ground the boy in ordinary life but the visual image blazes like a Gauguin painting. At the end, oracular comment of extraordinary intensity and power presents a despairing vision of the indifference of the universe and the annihilation waiting for all:

There is no home or resting place.
The broken ground will have us all
Indifferently back. And here he is,

Imprisoned in his element,
The angel boy who neither lives nor dies.
Where can his mother be? He waits among us,

Innocent and terrible. His smile is death,
And like the world his green-gold gaze
That should be love sees nothing everywhere.

In Embark, *Sean O'Brien deftly shifts between registers and tones to present and think about the world in different ways.*

131

Crucially, this vast annihilating vision is still anchored to the physical presence of the boy. The tension created between human sympathy and the bleak vision of cosmic indifference is what makes recognition of the latter so devastating.

A different beauty appears in the sardonically playful grace of the micropoems of 'Woodworks'. 'Rooks' is one:

The sitting tenants of the hilltop
keep a weather eye on everything.
Oh, they've heard it all before.
Surprise us, they say. Go on. Thought not.

The metaphor faces two ways: we see rooks as cynical, life-bruised people and people as cynical, life-bruised rooks. It's presented with the lightest, most humorous touch but implies both pathos and anger. It's the poet's reticence that makes the little poem so suggestive, inviting the reader's imagination to play around different ways of seeing the people and life-situations they evoke.

Such supple movement between different fields of knowledge or experience and reference, different levels of seriousness, different modes of address implying different relationships to the reader, is the fruit of many years' writing (this is apparently O'Brien's eleventh collection). It's also the fruit of many years' *reading*. The writing can be highly allusive, sometimes in ways declared on the surface, in references to figures like Rilke, Heaney, Heraclitus and Chateaubriand, Klee and Arcimboldo, or songs like the Grateful Dead's 'Box of Rain'. Often it's through quotations one may or may not recognise, quietly absorbed into the texture of O'Brien's own words. Such literariness is obviously deeply embedded in O'Brien's way of thinking. What's striking, though, is how tactfully he ensures that it's not a barrier to the less literary reader. There's an extreme example in the magnificent 'Waterworks'. This starts with a memorably phrased image of falling rain:

Indifferent to sorrow as to time,
the rain is bouncing off the outhouse roof

Actual rain and metaphorical analogues to it pervade the poem. In the middle comes the statement

Poor pelting slums and summer palaces
alike endure the rain

'Summer palaces' nods to Eliot's 'Journey of the Magi' but makes perfect sense on its own, in a world in which the homes of the super-rich effectively are palaces. 'Pelting slums' is given adequate meaning by the imagery of rain. However, for those who do pick up the reference to Edgar in Shakespeare's *King Lear* as he prepares to assume the role of the beggar Poor Tom and

                    from low farms,
Poor pelting villages, sheepcotes, and mills,
Sometime with lunatic bans, sometime with prayers,
Enforce their charity

there are further dimensions of richness. Above all, it invokes the play's concern with government and its violent contrasts of social justice and injustice, benevolence and cruelty, superfluity and deprivation – things that have been so much at issue in O'Brien's earlier books. They're less explicitly developed in this one, but pervasively implied in its background, and this poem contains a particularly sharp slash at government spin:

a mountainside collapses on a train

and we sit waiting for the minister to tell us
what's wrong now. We know he'll blame the rain
for raining and the poor for drawing breath

Throughout *Embark*, I warmed to O'Brien's gentle humanity. All the poems seemed to grow out of his concern for people, the emotions they feel and the lives they're given. Though steeped in high culture, sometimes framing his subjects in almost metaphysical anguish, he never sounded cerebral or remote. His stance towards the reader always implied a courteous

Though steeped in high culture, sometimes framing his subjects in almost metaphysical anguish, he never sounded cerebral or remote.

invitation to shared reflection.

Allowing for density of print, Gross's book probably contains well over twice as many words as O'Brien's. Its fertility in ideas, images and perceptions is almost breath-taking. So is the vivid precision of its language of physical description. The world it presents is above all crowded with movement. This is a part of the experience of modern life that Gross captures brilliantly. Glittering details seem to leap off every page. Looking down at a road at night the poet sees 'the cold blush of blue / on a cheek: stranger, her mobile tingling / with presence.' He sees road sweepers skirting round a nest of card-board boxes and bin sacks and thinks how 'From it, at dawn, / a man unfolded, straightened / what appeared to be a tie and walked away.' The teemingly mobile world of his poems involves the paradox that the storm of activity surrounding us is both alienating and a part of what we are. It's alienating because the sheer pace with which things change means we can't digest them intellectually, emotionally or imaginatively. At the same time, Gross has long been interested in exploring the porousness of the boundaries between us and the things around us. The long car-driving poem 'Smatter' develops this theme. In this quotation we see both the metrical skill that vivifies the hints of carnal contact in middle lines and the fundamentally cerebral and detached way in which the poet presents his material:

Could this in passing also
be a love song? Road is all
relationship, the traffic
between things, between
us. Breath, touch, word
and matter, the quiver and hum
even at night, the glow
behind the skyline. Road
is what connects us. Road
is appetite, and need.

In contrast with O'Brien's melancholy surveys of erosion and defeat, *The Thirteenth Angel* offers an almost continuous exultation in the sheer plenitude of life and a rejoicing in opulent language. Flamboyant titles in a style reminiscent of Wallace Stevens frame poems as High Art, perhaps with something of Stevens' own irony. Some, like 'Black Glass Sonata', 'Ash Plaint in the Key of O' or 'Descants on Dante', involve parallels between poetry and other art forms, usually music. Even without such explicit parallels, artifice may be proclaimed in a purely stylistic way. A long sequence inspired by lockdown is called 'Springtime in Pandemia', for example. And Gross frequently uses language that suggests religious transcendence. There's another paradox here though. Both verbal opulence and religious language seem to be intended not as escapes from humdrum reality but as ways of refreshing our perception of it. So the fifth section of the long 'Thirteen Angels' sequence starts with the title 'An Angel is a Kind of Music' and continues '*not that of the spheres but of the here and now*' (my italics).

Different styles, different costs and benefits. *Embark* and *The Thirteenth Angel* seem to me complementary in several ways.

For one thing, *Embark* makes us feel mentally and emotionally connected to the poet and the people he writes about. Its poetry is suffused with empathy. Less geared to connection on this level, *The Thirteenth Angel* explores the idea of connectedness as a flow of forces equally encompassing human and non-human being. For another, the polish of O'Brien's art appears in his verbal frugality and willingness to trust the reader, guiding responses with the lightest hints and suggestions. His line endings work as a way of relaxing the poet's control, giving breathing space to the reader's imagination. He carefully avoids overloading poems in a way that would fill these spaces. Gross is like Keats or Wallace Stevens in loading every rift with ore. Often cutting against the grain of the syntax to highlight shifts in his thought, his line endings tighten control over exactly how we read what he's written. This can seem oppressive. However, the desire to express and explore his material as exhaustively as possible is a source of his poetry's richness and intellectual power.

The teemingly mobile world of his poems involves the paradox that the storm of activity surrounding us is both alienating and a part of what we are.

133

Selima Hill's *Women in Comfortable Shoes* is different again. The poems are all short – many if not most six or fewer lines. They're grouped into sequences but even within these I think they largely work as separate units. They have the punchiness of epigrams but unlike epigrams what most offer is not pithy reflections on life in general but flashes of extremely subjective response to another person or to the speaker's immediate circumstances. She appears at different ages, as a child at home or a girl in a boarding school at one end of the book and as an old woman at the other. She comes across as highly intelligent and observant, vividly imaginative, prickly, rebellious and uncompromising, perpetually embattled with others and often conflicted in herself, bewildered by other people's feelings and behaviour and sometimes almost as much so by her own. In some ways this collection is like Hill's previous one – *Men Who Feed Pigeons* – but I felt that in *Men* the accumulation of impressions emerging between the lines of a given sequence encouraged me to achieve a sense of what the other characters in a relationship were like *in themselves*, independently of the poet-persona's reactions to them, and to 'read' her and their reactions in that wider context. I feel that much less in this collection.

Although their economy and clarity suggests the application of deliberate art, in other ways most of the very short poems have the air of immediate releases of thought, lightning flash spontaneity and truth to the impulse of the moment. This gives a sense of honesty and makes us – or made me – feel very close to the poet. It goes with a willingness to express unworthy feelings without shame or apparent self-consciousness. And it goes with a willingness to take artistic risks, plunging, for example, into images that may seem surreal but are actually vividly oblique expressions of conscious feeling, as in this portrait of a school prefect:

What I hated most were the clips
that lived and died in hundreds in her hair,

cascades of coloured clips with floral legs

incapable of understanding anything.

In a book so full of subversive energy and arresting moments it's hard to pick out particular examples – I'd probably go for different ones every time I tried to make a choice – but I was particularly impressed by 'Curd' from the sequence 'Susan and Me'. This describes a vulnerable school friend who apparently suffers mental collapse as an adult:

When I see her in the threadbare dressing gown
somebody has wrapped her in like curd,

the gentle face that wishes it was air
now pressed against the wall, I lose my nerve

and walk away in tears, having witnessed
something I am not prepared to bear.

The overwhelming pathos of this is freed from any hint of sentimentality or suggestion that the poet is trying to pressurize the reader both by the deadpan nature of the 'like curd' simile and by the honesty with which Hill admits that in the end the most important thing to her is protecting herself from her own grief.

... Hill admits that in the end the most important thing to her is protecting herself from her own grief.

About the Author

Edmund Prestwich lives in Manchester and taught for many years at the Manchester Grammar School. He is the author of two collections and reviews poetry for several magazines.

PAM THOMPSON

Peter Raynard, *Manland,* 81pp, £9.99, Nine Arches Press

Clare Shaw, *Towards a General Theory of Love,* 79pp, £10.99, Bloodaxe Books Ltd.

Olive Senior, *Hurricane Watch: New and Collected Poems,* 451pp, £25.00, Carcanet

---

Peter Raynard's second collection can be positioned with other recent books that explore the complex dynamics of masculinity, such as those by Andrew McMillan and Lewis Buxton. Raynard, editor of the online journal, *Proletarian Poetry*, is a disabled working class poet from Coventry. At the end of the 'seventies, the personal and the political collided when Midlands bands combined reggae beats with a social conscience. In 'On Hearing Racist Chants at a Steel Pulse Gig' recalls the interruption of the teenage Raynard's enjoyment the music by those racist chants. Each couplet has its own raging beat, imitating emotions of anger, pride, fear and impotence:

I stop walking on the spot, fifteen-year-old
petrified punk   soap-spiked hair

no holler & ball to shoulder blade them all.
Shaming my city of peace once blitzed

by the Nazis. Skinny little white boy
I wish violence was my intention

There is an undercurrent of violence in the poems; a catalogue of micro- and not-so-micro, aggressions committed by men. Raynard does not let himself off the hook. He is as complicit as the next man in being goaded by the toxic pressures of masculinity to square up and not want to back down in the face of a fight. In 'mano a mano', the pantoum's repetitions are ideal for conveying the push-pull urge of the speaker to react and to not react to another man's provocation:

The man thinks he's being the reasonable man
as he holds me back, dishing out grief
with his son saying 'leave it dad, not again'
a verbal stab into his dad's beliefs.

...

My moving hand becomes a fisted charge

so a normal life can't be about me on a march
trying to talk him down so I won't find
my moving hand becoming a fisted charge.

The skilfully-managed variations to the syntax, rhythm and rhyming ensure that the movement of the poem is dynamic and not merely circular.

Reynard is an astute observer and social commentator; he speaks both for himself and for those who are likely to be 'othered' in being called 'service-users'. The poems' subjects, and their narratives, are made distinctive via varied linguistic and formal structures that contrast with the heartless jargon of the bureaucracy surrounding benefits and social care. The prose poem, 'Violence Decides', has an epigraph from Mahatma Ghandi, *'Poverty is the worst form of violence'*:

Violence draws
up a personal independence plan   for the alcoholic
so soaked it gets him a job behind the bar as an optic.
Violence is the Order Paper pointing questions
towards
an obfuscation of meetings   greetings and
beatings.

The lengthened spaces between words slows down the reading and gives certain words/phrases added emphasis. Violence is personified as a tyrannical infiltrator of social functions and institutions and might be missed as such if not for poems like these.

Jacqueline Saphra writes in the blurb that *Manland* is " Part manifesto, part hymn, part raging lament", a good summation of its various tones. It is heartfelt, stark and brutally honest, about mental health issues, and the silences and shame surrounding them. 'What

Reynard is an astute observer and social commentator; he speaks both for himself and for those who are likely to be 'othered' in being called 'service-users'.

the Older Men Tell Each Other about their Depression' heads a blank page. 'Swimming Away in Circles' is a sequence of twelve poems, which Reynard says in the Notes, 'are loosely based', on an Institute of Psychiatry Research project he was involved in on the North Peckham estate in the 1990s. The sequence is bookended by 'before' and 'after' poems about the recruiting of interviewees and the findings. The setting, a block of flats where researchers post leaflets offering '£10 to partake' is bleak. 'The tenth-floor corridors would make Kafka chuck / his book against death-row doors.' ('Recruiting Interviewees'). Ten of the poems – with sonnet-frameworks – are based on interviews that took place on the ground floor of the flats, with mostly, but not all, men. They tell of substance-abuse, disability, self-harm, mental and physical displacement. Fragile facades prevail, sometimes with a hauntingly surreal edge – a young woman turns up with 'her shiny floor Mother   whose at a loss / to find answers to her past' (6. 'The Mother's Ghost') Is it the daughter or the mother, though, or both, who are 'ghostly'? Each is lost to the other. For the disabled man, 'life is a septic in-growing toenail', a daily round of prescribed and non-prescribed medications, 'waiting on a change that spits // on you from a devastating height of hope.' (9. The Disabled Man'). Alternate stanzaic end-rhymes and rhyming couplets give a dissonant jauntiness to these narratives of grim lives – the final poem in the sequence is a kind of summation, not to be trite but to be deadly serious, that the results of the research yield no surprises and no solutions, 'This census of people   told all is commercial / hear Kafka laugh   as they swim away in circles'. ('The Findings')

Reynard examines parenthood, specifically in a series of poems, interspersed through the collection, about a stay-at-home dad. These are rueful, sardonic, humorous and tender; there is a sense, overall, that Home-Father cannot find a way to adjust to the role and that society does not allow for such an adjustment. He perceives that other parents possess a sense of purpose that he feels is lacking in his own life:

Plagued with elegance, Home-Mothers arrive en-masse
recounting midday errands, after-school plans.

Sleep-filled Bengali Fathers have risen
to pick up kids before heading out

to deposit various people in various states
of inebriation across various places of this earth.
     ('Home-Father's School Daze')

Memories are triggered of his own school-days, when children flew out of school like birds and he 'remembers running / towards his own Mother with a flock / of hunger beside him   chirping   singing'. The last of this series of poems, 'Home-Father: A King in Waiting', addressed to his son, recalls a succession of 'Waits', 'The Waits began at birth, tiny yellow body six days / in neo-natal', and further on:

in a car I had to keep ticking over
to keep warm. Snow white field, a risky adventure

looking back, how we let you camp on a winter's night
shows up the decisions we made to assuage your
     depression.

This is a gorgeous poems with its candid recollections and assured rhythms. Its social and cultural references puts it, and us, in the 'there and then' and the 'here and now': A&E, Heaney's *Death of a Naturalist*, Descartes, Xbox, 'the jab', history having since overtaken the events of its conclusion:
     Bob Marley's *I'm Still Waiting* on repeat. Like the old soak

Charles, I have waited to long, time to hand me my crown.

Peter Reynard reports from manhood's frontline with insight into the callous bureaucracies which neutralize mental illness, disability and poverty. Each stanza of 'A

Sestina to Die For' is a different slant on the filling-in of a questionnaire to apply for benefits. The form of the poem once more suits its subject, with repeated line end-words returning with numbing circularity, some hitting particularly hard, 'the digital triage you will face', 'How long has it now / been since you have decided to be disabled?' 'This mime must end'. In the coda, the 'no reply' from the claimant, returns us chillingly to the poem's title.

Manland is not a comforting read but neither is it comfortless because Reynard has paid such close attention to rhythm, sound patterning and musicality, has varied his forms with good reason, and, in writing affecting poems about his own childhood, shows the oscillation between man and boy. For all of the above, love permeates *Manland*: instances when it was desperately sought but not found, was never know, or could never be expressed, or its potential was trampled because of traps of class, poverty and illness.

Clare Shaw's fourth collection is about different kinds of love and what happens when we lose someone we love or are deprived of it altogether. The title draws on a psychiatric study, *A General Theory of Love* by Thomas Louis, Fari Amini and Richard Lannon, about the complexities of love and its place in human wellbeing. It is also underpinned by the another study, by psychologist, Harry Harlow, *Total social isolation in monkeys*, which refers to his controversial experiments in the 1950s which proved the lasting detrimental effects of maternal deprivation on baby rhesus monkeys, and on their mothers.

The opening poem sets the tone, for teachings about love, and where to find them:

Wolf says howl for it. Die for it.
Monkey goes mad for the lack of it.
　　('What the Frog Taught Me About Love')

From animals, rather than humans, it would seem. The first quarter of the book contains poems in memory of Shaw's mother and grandmother and also celebrates the birth and early life of the poet's daughter, 'And you ask, would I die for you? / A thousand times over.' ('Child Protection Policy'). Shaw express inexpressible grief in various ways. 'Letter to My Mother', a prose poem, is a letter addressed to the mother on the brink of death.

Just tell me about yourself, the things that
matter: how many skips of a stone you could
　　　　　make on the water;
the roses; the nameless trees. Let's leave all the
　　　　　bad stuff to
one side.

It is intimate and urgent, made more so by Shaw's skill with rhythm and half-rhyme.

In 'abcedarian', language breaks down, like the mother's, with her 'cerebrovascular / disease and risk factors' and so does the poet's in this modelling of aphasia by means of staggered white space and elisions of words.

i don't have a　map and　　　　　　when you can't
join th. e dots　there is no cure
kiddo　all you have
　left is dots　she was my
　　mother no story can hold this　　　the decli
ne happened stepby step and
　　ogoditwasterrible

Shaw's language is not complicated, and the images – predominantly of nature – moon, stars, sky, wind, rain, snow, flowers, birds, sunlight, soil – universal. They avoid becoming clichéd tropes of lyric poetry because of their close associations with human emotions of grief, love, and also joy, and gain mythic status In being repeated. Many of these these poems were written during the pandemic – some more overtly than others – when our relation to the natural world was heightened as the human world quietened down. Two poems, set side by side, take different approaches. 'Love as a Global Pandemic', a list poem in nine tercets, juxtaposes the frightening and the tender; the lies of politicians, the desperation and the hope, 'Love as

Shaw's language is not complicated, and the images – predominantly of nature – moon, stars, sky, wind, rain, snow, flowers, birds, sunlight, soil – universal.

keeping your distance, love as prayer / love a park you can't sit in, love as birds'.

It reminds us how it was and how strange and unlikely that time seems now. In contrast 'What the Moon Taught Me About Love', a moon seen during lockdown prompts personal memories of Shaw's childhood at Christmas, 'a perfect moon / the night outside complete and endless / and we sing because the grown-ups tell us / that Santa will hear us.' The moon in childhood denotes innocence and expectation but the same moon, in the spring of 2020, reflects the sense of isolation:

and the bees getting fat but the ducks going hungry
and the sky is painfully blue and empty
and the lambs are growing up fast
and the weeks are months but the hours pass quickly
... .

And the moon tonight is very lonely

Listing, use of anaphora, a tender command of cadence: on the page, the poems carry the charge of Shaw's reading voice.

Threaded throughout are poems as conversations between the poet/narrator and the character, Monkey. But who is Monkey? Monkey represents all the monkeys in Harry Harlow's cruel experiments who have been separated from their mothers and who grieve for the loss. Monkey is also Clare Shaw's spirit animal, is anima/animus. The poems chart the poet's and Monkey's psychological and spiritual – in the widest sense – journey. It is painful, conventional religion is no help, and sets no example. God, 'is cruel in the name of love', and 'He throws his own son in a pit'. Better to write your own tale, as Monkey does, which is terrifying too

His poems are sharp wires
and they sting.

The words are small paws
They leave a trail of blood across the page

And the mess is terrible.
    ('Monkey Writes a Story About God')

The final line implores Monkey, 'Now turn the page'.

Shaw is an advocate for women and children who have experienced trauma. Self injury comes in many forms and there is both seriousness and a lightness of touch in 'Monkey Talks About Self Injury', 'When he bites himself, he says, he belongs to a tradition / dating back thousands of years.' The premise is poet as therapist, 'though he understands the desire / to express grief, he is easily triggered. // Liposuction distresses him terribly, as do piercings ... / We have not discussed waxing, but he is aware of sunbeds and bleachings.'

Shaw's last collection, *Flood* (2018), was written at a time when their home town of Hebden Bridge was destroyed by floods. Poems of personal loss and mental illness were aligned with that devastation. Snow features significantly in these newer poems, one reason being, according to Shaw, was a move out of the valley into the hills. Falling snow connects back to stories and childhood bringing both a forgetting and remembering, 'Somewhere, there's another world / behind a door you've been knocking on / since you were young.' ('The Chronicles of Narnia), and 'I want to stay the kind of person / who finds snow beautiful, / even when I fall.' ('If Love is Snow')

Clare Shaw admits that dialogues with Monkey are largely self-dialogues and that by the end of the collection recognizes that they have become Monkey, and there is peace, of sorts.

When you come late to snow,

Says Monkey, you will always be ready
to stand under the moon
to watch it fall.
Sometimes I don't know which of us

is Monkey.
    ('Monkey Invites Me to Imagine')

Shaw is an advocate for women and children who have experienced trauma.

The opening poem with its lessons about love being learnt from animals, connects with the final poem, 'Monkey Reads William Blake'. According to Monkey,

> ... Blake is part monkey
> and John Clare, with his exquisitely sensitive eye.
> Dogs, he says, are also half monkey.

Like Monkey, Blake 'hated the cage so much / he rid his brain of it', and he and the poet, as one, do this by writing:

> the dogs are all howling
> the two of us dancing
> and Monkey is grinning.

Theory is all very well, and Shaw, is aware of its place, but also of its limitations in relation to the lives of the grieving and the lost. This is poetry of feeling which is never sentimental. The poet speaks their truths and makes them ours.

Olive Senior is the poet laureate of Jamaica and *Hurricane Watch: New and Collected Poems* brings together poems from her first four collections. The volume is arranged reverse chronological order, beginning with poems from the 2007 collection, *Shells*, moving through *Over the Roofs of the World* (2005), *Gardening in the Tropics* (1994), *Talking of Trees* (1985) along with a selection of *New and Uncollected* poems, which forms the final section. I had come across Senior's vivid and alert poems before but it was a treat to read her more extensively and get a sense of her development. The first thing that struck me that you wouldn't necessarily know which were earlier or later poems as the treatment of her themes of Jamaican ecology, politics and culture is consistently clear and engaging.

Early poems dwell on home, family and local landscape of childhood. The poet looks back on her growing up, having moved away to a Canadian city. There is a sense that lives of men and women took different paths. In 'Birdshooting Season', 'the men / make marriages of their guns', while 'long contentless women / stir their brews', and make provisions, 'wrap pone and tie-leaf / for tomorrow's sport.'

The guns foreshadow 'large dark wings / like War' in 'Cockpit County Dreams', an interruption to the young girl's carefreeness, her 'mountain-goat' plunging:

> Planes bringing bombs, said my father
> Babies, said my mother
> (Portents of a split future).
>   (I)

Senior's mother shows her daughter photos of black ancestors, 'Herein / your ancestry, your imagery, your pride.' (II) Both mother and father entreat her to know and study rivers. She concludes that her 'disorder of ancestry / proves as stable as the many rivers / flowing around me.' yet says 'Undocumented / I drown in the other's history'. (III) Knowledge of ancestry comes to the child in many ways, the mother's 'harvesting' of childbirth, the father lulling her to sleep, in his rituals of planting; in expected prayers. Male violence is prevalent in the poems, whether within the family, 'the whiplash of my / father's wrath' or from colonisers and plunderers. The child's first acts of freedom are a refusal to pray and an attempt to break away from binding ancestral myths though, as an adult, the poet feels the pull of both:

> Now against the rhythms
> of subway trains my
> heartbeats still drum
> worksongs. Some wheels
> sing freedom. The others
> Home.
>   (IV)

In 'Colonial Girl's School', the poet addresses a childhood friend in a poem which is almost like a song with a refrain, 'There was nothing about ourselves / There was nothing about us at all', which changes very slightly on each repetition. There is a disconnect when the girls were being taught Shakespeare, Latin declensions

The poet looks back on her growing up, having moved away to a Canadian city.

and about the Kings and Queens of England when the political events remained unmentioned:

'Thirty-eight was a beacon. A flame.
They were talking of desegregation
in Little Rock, Arkansas. Lumumba
And the Congo. To us: mumbo-jumbo.
We *had* read Vachel Lindsay's
Vision of the jungle.

The friends, one day, would compare stories, 'How the mirror broke / Who kissed us awake / Who let Anansi from his bag'.

Senior writes poems that attempt to reckon with the legacy of slavery, the story of the man, a former slave, 'who grew up to be / somebody's / grandfather', tells the child who asks, 'Where we come from?', 'Anansi / leapt from the bag ...' ('Anansi's 'tory') Reclaiming ancestral stories is an act of visibility and pride but Senior recognises that these can become smokescreens to difficult realities, and means for white people to allow stereotypes and prejudice to continue. In the second part of the poem, the poet/speaker, watches 'the legless / beggar on wheels' in a street in Kingston, Jamaica and counts her fortunes but it is an uneasy gratitude:

But what's the use of legs if you're
burdened with a mind
rushing headlong into dark
endings said the shadow

The contrast between the urban and rural is a thread running through Senior's work but nature is not romanticised nor are cities presented as wholly 'bad'. The poet draws attention to her own privilege and the complexities in presenting different environments and their inhabitants. 'Nature Studies I' and 'II' are dialogues between a poet and a 'lover' - I wondered if the 'lover' was the island of Jamaica. The lover 'embraces mountains', gives advice, 'do not write life poems // the worm / will / hear you.// Make a compass of your

mind ... // Learn from nature', which the poet resists and 'writes a life poem':

the poem
self-destructs

the worm

devours the mountain

Is a 'life' poem too grandiose and impossible? Or, if, about one person's life, too limited? Is this like Blake's worm, a symbol of sickness and death? In the second part, the poet /speaker conveys her own restless body and mind:

III
Hard like dogs or adolescents the mountains
Range in packs there is no escaping them, it's not
The mountains that move it's your perspective you
             laugh
Forgetting how in the cockpits of my endless
voyagings and your landlocked imaginings

        I lost mine.

The poem ends in resolution of sorts, as the 'poet', for now, moves more towards the 'lover's' position, saying 'one day / mountains will come / clear / as mirrors', allowing passage through them 'to the point where mountain roots / intersect // all life.'

But, of course, Senior is anything but solipsistic as her poems give voice and speak to and of so many different people of different ages, backgrounds and social class.

The selection of poems from *Gardening in the Tropics* (1994) begins with 'Meditation on Yellow', one of two Meditations on a colour (the other, on Red, is addressed to Jean Rhys, 'You, voyager / in the dark'), where 'yellow' represents the plundered 'gold', literal or metaphorical, of 'El Dorado', the Caribbean islands but also what was taken or corrupted 'the yellow dawn of our innocence'. The poem is in sections, the speaker, multi-voiced, (e.g.

The contrast between the urban and rural is a thread running through Senior's work but nature is not romanticised nor are cities presented as wholly 'bad'.

as a worker in various types of labour), to an addressee, 'you', who could be both a modern-day tourist or historical 'explorer'. The concluding words are defiant:

> you cannot tear my song
> from my throat
>
> you cannot erase the memory
> of my story

Four poems contain stories of hurricanes in 1901, 1944, 1951 and 1988, and others, again in a section of 'Nature Studies', feature local plants beginning with a poem called 'Plants', which, while celebrating the natural world's abundance and tenacity, is done so via the conceit of colonisation, 'a sinister not to say imperialistic // grand design.'

> The world is full of shoots bent on conquest,
> invasive seedlings seeking wide open spaces,
> matériel gathered for explosive dispersal
> In capsules and seed cases.

This is humour with serious intent preparing the reader for the consistently ironic tone of the sequence of twelve poems, 'Gardening in the Tropics' where each poem begins with the phrase 'Gardening in the Tropics ...' which perhaps sounds like an idyllic pastime but all too often it precedes descriptions of acts of violence, political corruption and environmental and ecological damage such as the government's getting rid of a productive mixed farming system and, consequently, livelihoods too ('The Knot Garden').

The first poem, 'Brief Lives, begins:

> Gardening in the Tropics, you never know
> what you'll turn up. Quite often, bones.
> 　　　 ... the skulls of *desparecidos* —
> the disappeared ones.

Jackie Wills features this poem in her excellent, *On Poetry: Reading, Writing and Working with Poems*

(Smith|Doorstop, 2022) and where she discusses her own experience of gardening, and the importance of 'ground'. She quotes from a lecture Senior gave in Canada in 2019.

> Real gardening can expose not just dirt but secrets and memories, as can poetry, it's a way to explore the significance of ground as repository of those who came before us.
> 　(p.38)

The poem features the skeleton of a young man who, 'crossed the invisible boundary into rival political territory.', and 'the drug baron / wiped out in territorial competition', and Wills draws attention to the poem's timelessness in its relevance to drug-dealing and territorial consequences of transgression today.

The poems, characteristically, adopt various forms and voices. 'Gardening on the Run' is spoken by a dead runaway slave, called, 'runaway, maroon, cimarron.' 'Marronage' was the act of extricating oneself from slavery; the penalty, torture and eventual death. The poem is harrowing in the savagery the speaker experienced before death, freedom after death being preferable to earthly servitude, and the voice of the monologue is once again one of defiance:

> 　 I've found
> no matter what you were
> recording of plantations and
> settlements, we could not be
> mitted. We are always there
> like some dark stain in your
> diaries and notebooks, your
> letters, your court records,
> your law books — as if we had
> ambushed your pen.

Wills draws attention to a detailed glossary of 'Gardening in the Tropics' online which includes descriptions of plants named in the poems as well as explanations of words and history.

Wills draws attention to a detailed glossary of 'Gardening in the Tropics' online which includes descriptions of plants named in the poems as well as explanations of words and history.

This seems an appropriate place to draw to a conclusion a review of a weighty *Collected* whose surface I feel I've hardly skimmed. *Shell* (2007) contains photographs and drawings. There are more monologues, of the non-human, a snail, a chick in an egg (a concrete poem shaped like an egg), an ear of maize, a field of sugar-cane:

It is not so much the shell shock as questions
we never asked that leave us cowering still
among the dead sugar metaphors.
('Canefield Surprised by Emptiness')

The word 'shell' returns and reverberates meaning, at once, protection, fragility, vulnerability, wealth (mother-of-pearl). *New and Uncollected Poems* revisit some of the earlier themes: experiences of childhood, poverty, drought, stolen crops, violent deaths, like that of a child caught in the crossfire of a gang shooting in where modern technology provides a further layer of intrusiveness:

And the child of ten leans over with her cell phone
camera
to take a picture of her classmate in the coffin
and a picture of the child taking a picture of her
classmate in the coffin
(draped with a cloth reading: Stacey-Anne Gone
Too Soon)
ends up on the front news of the newspaper. Of what
us it that?

Another question the poet/speaker asks is 'Where do we go from here?'. In one way or another, Olive Senior has been asking that throughout her poetic career.

About the Author

Pam Thompson's collections include *Show Date and Time*, chosen by Simon Armitage as a winner of the Poetry Business Competition, and *Strange Fashion* from Pindrop Press.

INDEX OF POETS AND POEMS